THE PRINCIPLES OF ASTROLOGY

Charles E. O. Carter achieved a world-wide reputation as an astrologer through his many lectures, articles, and books. He was President of the Astrological Lodge in London for 30 years, editor of the magazine, *Astrology*, Patron of the Astrological Association (research), and Principal Emeritus of the Faculty of Astrological Studies which has taught the ancient science to thousands of students in 75 countries.

The Principles of Astrology gives a clear, concise presentation of modern astrology permeated by the author's spiritual approach, which gives depth and unity to his writing. In one easily understood chapter, the student is shown how to erect the horoscope; the fundamental nature of the Signs, Planets, Houses, and Aspects is explained in such a manner that he is enabled to integrate these varied and often conflicting factors into a sound judgment. A good index makes reference easy.

Mr. Carter claims—and proves from a lifetime of practical study—that whatever the aspects may be in any instance, "all things work together for the highest good of all beings". Without preaching, he indicates the relationship of man to himself, to his brothers, and to the cosmos as shown in the horoscope, thus providing a rational and meaningful pattern for living.

THE PRINCIPLES OF ASTROLOGY

By

Charles E. O. Carter

PRESIDENT EMERITUS OF THE ASTROLOGICAL LODGE
FIRST PRINCIPAL OF THE FACULTY OF
ASTROLOGICAL STUDIES

AUTHOR OF
"THE ENCYCLOPAEDIA OF PSYCHOLOGICAL ASTROLOGY"
"THE ZODIAC AND THE SOUL"
"SYMBOLIC DIRECTIONS IN MODERN ASTROLOGY"
"SOME PRINCIPLES OF HOROSCOPIC DELINEATION"
"ESSAYS ON THE FOUNDATIONS OF ASTROLOGY"
"THE ASTROLOGY OF ACCIDENTS"
"ASTROLOGICAL ASPECTS"

A QUEST BOOK
Published under a grant from The Kern Foundation

THE THEOSOPHICAL PUBLISHING HOUSE
Wheaton, Ill., U.S.A.

Madras, India / London, England

First edition 1925
Second ,, 1931
Third ,, 1939
Fourth ,, 1952
Fifth and revised edition 1963
Reprinted 1969

© Theosophical Publishing House Ltd.

Quest Book edition 1971 published by The Theosophical Publishing House, Wheaton, Illinois, a department of The Theosophical Society in America, by arrangement with The Theosophical Publishing House Ltd.

Second Quest Book printing 1972

ISBN: 0-8356-0423-3

Library of Congress Catalog Number: 79-154829

Printed in the United States of America

FOREWORD

THE present work is designed to give a clear and concise presentation of the essential facts of modern Astrology.

A good deal of experience in teaching the average beginner has convinced me that, while there are several text-books suitable for the use of the more advanced student or of a novice who has the advantage of personal tuition, the majority are either too prolix or too condensed for one who is compelled to be his own instructor. Moreover, Astrology is now to some extent in the melting-pot: on the one hand, many new ideas are being introduced; on the other, statistical research, such as earlier astrologers could not carry out for lack of sufficient data, has cast considerable doubt on the validity of portions of the rather incoherent mass of tradition that till recent years represented astrological science.

The beginner does not wish to be confronted with controversial matters, however attractive he may find them later. He requires, firstly, a statement of what may be regarded as known astrological facts; and secondly, an explanation as to how these facts affect human life. It is this that I have aimed at giving him.

An endeavour is made not to neglect the theoretical aspects of Astrology, for the modern student dislikes what appear to him as isolated statements, and looks for a logical and synthetic aspect to our teaching, without, of course, wishing to plunge at the outset into metaphysical speculation.

I trust that the Index will be of considerable use in practice, since it should enable the student to find readily those passages that deal with any matter that may trouble him.

Finally, I would express my sincere hope that this book may be of some value in assisting its readers to grasp something of the true nature and worth of astrological science, both in the commonest and the most sublime aspects of human life. Those who have realized what this may mean to the individual are reluctant to set any bounds to their estimate of the beneficial effects that its universal recognition, in a proper form, would mean to the human race.

CHARLES E. O. CARTER

February, 1925.

FOREWORD TO THE SECOND EDITION

THIS edition represents a careful revision of the former text, and, besides many minor alterations, some substantial additions have been made, chiefly in Chapter Two.

Brevity is necessary in order to keep to a price that all can pay, but I have tried to avoid any sacrifice of lucidity, or, within the scope of the book, of completeness.

My chief desire has been to keep a sense of proportion, throwing the main principles into bold relief, for, if these are once comprehended, the particulars will be easily assimilated.

Chapter Ten has been augmented with sections on Symbolic Directions and on Rectification.

It would hardly be human to feel no pleasure in contemplating the many friends this work has made for me in the most diverse parts of the world which I can never hope to visit in the flesh. I trust that this fresh edition will continue the activities of its forerunner and spread the wonderful illumination of astrological knowledge ever further afield.

CHARLES E. O. CARTER

October, 1930.

FOREWORD TO THE THIRD EDITION

THE publication of a third edition of this work has enabled me to make a careful revision of the whole, to make certain alterations in the text and a few additions which will, I hope, be of the nature of improvements. On the whole, however, the book remains unchanged.

CHARLES E. O. CARTER

August, 1939.

FOREWORD TO THE FOURTH EDITION

THIS embodies many alterations and additions which, it is hoped, constitute improvements. In particular Chapter Two has been largely re-written; and in this connection the author acknowledges with thanks much help from Mr. George H. Bailey of Bath.

The Chapter on Horary and Electional Astrology has been omitted since it seemed best to restrict the work to Natal Astrology. Once this boundary is overstepped there seems no reason why the horary branch should be included and not chapters upon each of the several other special fields of astrological science, and this would obviously swell the book to twice or thrice its present size and quite alter its character.

In the main it has seemed right to present the traditional astrological teaching; and where I have deviated from it, this has been indicated by appropriate language.

It is now a quarter of a century since the "Principles" first appeared and in this period the Great Science has made strides towards general recognition such as could scarcely have been foreseen in 1925. Some labour all their lives for unpopular causes and die without seeing any measurable result for their strivings. It has been my happy lot to witness, if not the triumph of astrological truth, at least very great progress towards that consummation.

CHARLES E. O. CARTER

Winter, 1950.

FOREWORD TO THE FIFTH EDITION

A NUMBER of minor alterations, and some more important additions, will be found in this revised edition.

It is really not possible to produce, in this form, anything like a survey of all the principal methods employed by modern astrologers. For instance, there is a not inconsiderable school of "sidereal" astrology, employing the zodiac of the constellations in place of the tropical or equinoctial circle.

Such things were hardly known in the West in 1925 when this text-book first appeared and it is best to refer any that may be interested in such developments to works that deal specifically with them. To treat them briefly and inadequately would be unfair from all points of view.

In my belief the most important addition is that upon page 162 on the value of the winter ingress, and had space been available, I would have liked to expand this. Certainly I would, for myself, never think of judging either a nativity or a directional survey without reference to the preceding Capricorn ingress.

CHARLES E. O. CARTER

Autumn, 1962.

CONTENTS

ASTROLOGY AND ITS SUBJECT-MATTER

§ 1. INTRODUCTORY

ASTROLOGY is the science of certain cryptic relations between the celestial bodies and terrestrial life.

Natal Astrology is the study of these relations in regard to human life.

Furthermore, Astrology is a practical science, for it teaches us how to apply the information that it imparts to our personal and social life. Also, it is an Art, for the delineation of the Nativity, or Horoscope of Birth, calls into play faculties allied to the artistic.

It lays no claim to be what used to be called an "exact" science, but studies certain predispositions or tendencies in human life, which are sometimes indicated so clearly that they become virtual certainties.

The uses of Astrology are manifold, and its scope is limited only by the bounds of human life in its widest extent. The following aspects of the science may be mentioned:

Philosophical: It endeavours to set forth a coherent and scientifically verifiable scheme of cosmic manifestation.

Ethical: It traces the interactions between the Cosmos and the human mind and soul, and studies the true nature of what are called good and evil. It gives understanding of ourselves and others, and consequently broadens the sympathies and enlarges the outlook.

Spiritual and Religious: It endeavours to understand the essential nature of the divine ordinances and the ministers of divine power, in so far as is humanly possible.

Practical: By explaining the operations of cosmic laws it enables us to adapt our lives to them, and to advise and assist others to make the most of their lives, without waste of time and effort.

On the other hand, it must be borne in mind that our knowledge of Astrology is very far from complete. It is still studied by comparatively few, and it is overlaid with the growth of centuries of ignorance and charlatanism.

Astrology does not involve any form of psychism, and is founded upon mathematical and astronomical data, interpreted according to general principles.

It would be premature, at this stage and in a work of this nature, to discuss whether the heavenly bodies affect us directly as causative agents, or whether there is simply a correspondence between their motions and positions and the natures and destinies of human races and individuals. There may be truth in both views.

Astrologers commonly talk of the "effects" or "influences" of the planets and speak of such and such a position having produced or caused a certain effect. Such language (which in practice is not easily avoided) must not be taken as implying a belief in direct stellar causation, at any rate in the present work.

Practical experiment will soon convince the most sceptical that the bodies of the solar system indicate, if they do not actually produce, changes in:

1. Our minds.
2. Our feelings and emotions.
3. Our physical bodies.
4. Our external affairs and relationships with the world at large.

Astrology studies, as its subject-matter, four chief categories:

1. The Sun, Moon, and Planets.
2. The Zodiac.
3. The Houses of the Horoscope.
4. The Planetary Aspects.

We may mention, further, the Fixed Stars, whose value, at least so far as the individual is concerned, is questioned by many, and Sensitive Points, which, except the Part of Fortune, are beyond the scope of an introductory work.

In this chapter it is proposed to explain in a general sense what each of these four categories is, treating them in detail in subsequent chapters.

§ 2

The Sun, Moon, and Planets comprise the main elements of our Solar System, or Sun-System. The Sun is a star, like others that one sees on a clear night; and all the planets, of which the earth is one, revolve round it in their "orbits", while most, if not all, planets have satellites or moons which revolve round them.[1] The earth has one satellite—our Moon; the satellites of the other planets possess no known astrological importance. The fixed stars are immensely farther from us than even the most distant planet.

The Sun is indicated by the symbol ☉ and the Moon by ☽, and the planets and their symbols are as follows, counting from the Sun outwards:

Mercury	.	.	.	.	.	☿
Venus	.	.	.	.	.	♀
(The Earth)	.	.	.	.	—
Mars	.	.	.	.	.	♂
Jupiter	.	.	.	.	.	♃
Saturn	.	.	.	.	.	♄
Uranus	.	.	.	.	.	♅
Neptune	.	.	.	.	.	♆
Pluto			(not yet determined)			

The Earth can hardly be studied astrologically, for the reason that its value must necessarily be the same for all of us. It is our

[1] ☿ and ♀ have no known satellites.

station at which we receive the rays of the other planets as they circle around the Sun with it, in ever-changing mutual relations.

Uranus and Neptune were discovered in modern times; the others have been known from remote ages. Pluto was discovered in 1930.

The Sun and Moon are commonly called the *Lights* or *Luminaries*.

Venus and Jupiter are traditionally called the lesser and greater *benefics*, and Mars and Saturn the lesser and greater *malefics*.

By the adherents of some schools of thought, it has been objected that it is incorrect to apply these terms to any planets. Nevertheless they are in practice highly convenient. When well placed the benefics indicate easy fortunes and the more social and brighter virtues; the malefics, success by hard work and the harder and more worldly-useful qualities. Under serious afflictions the benefics cause the less grave misfortunes and such failings as indolence and extravagance, which make a man his own enemy rather than actively harmful to others; the malefics in such circumstances may occasion dangerous conditions and an unfortunate or even malignant disposition.[1]

Uranus and Neptune incline somewhat to the malefic character. The Sun, Moon, and Mercury depend greatly for the nature of their action on their special positions in each horoscope. They are termed *Neutrals*. The nature of Pluto is still a matter for investigation.

A group of three or more bodies within a few degrees of one another is called a *Satellitium* (plural, *Satellitia*).

§ 3. The Signs of the Zodiac

Astrological philosophy teaches that visible nature (at least so far as we are able to observe it) arises from the interaction of what are called the four *Elements*[2] (or *Triplicities*[3]), symbolically

[1] Such statements as the above may sound fatalistic. It is impossible at every stage in a text-book, to guard against expressions which may to some ears have this implication, but the reader is referred to the last chapter for a note on this problem and its relations to Astrology.

[2] Not, of course, to be confused with the chemical elements of modern physics.

[3] The word Trigon is also sometimes employed.

named Fire, Air, Earth, and Water, and the three *Qualities* (Quadruplicities) or modes of action, named the Cardinal, Fixed, and Mutable. These seven principles are presumably cosmic, or universal, whereas the Sun, Moon, and Planets are of course finite existences within our Solar System. We have no reason to suppose that other solar systems are counterparts of our own: indeed, it is certain that they are not. But there is no reason to suppose that the Elements and Qualities are merely local.

The *Zodiac* is the pathway of the Sun, Moon, and planets, and lies like a belt round the earth. It is invisible, and we can only detect its position by noticing where the planets are at night, just as one can trace the course of a distant road at night by watching the lights of the traffic passing along it. The fixed stars are not limited to the zodiac; as we can see for ourselves they are scattered over the entire sky. Some lie in the Zodiac, such as Antares, Aldebaran, Castor and Pollux, and Regulus; others do not.

At all times and places half the zodiac lies above the horizon and half below.

It is divided into twelve *Signs*, each containing 30 degrees (written °), making 360 degrees in all.

Each Degree is divided into 60 Minutes (written ') and each Minute into 60 Seconds (written ").

Note that these symbols (' and ") are applicable to minutes and seconds of *longitude*. Minutes and seconds of *time* are abbreviated as m. and s.

The Latin and English names of these twelve signs, with their symbols, are as follows:

1.	Aries the Ram	♈
2.	Taurus the Bull	♉
3.	Gemini the Twins	♊
4.	Cancer the Crab	♋

5.	Leo the Lion	.	.	.	.	♌
6.	Virgo the Maiden	.	.	.	.	♍
7.	Libra the Scales	.	.	.	.	♎
8.	Scorpio the Scorpion	.	.	.	.	♏
9.	Sagittarius the Archer	.	.	.	.	♐
10.	Capricorn the He-Goat	.	.	.	.	♑
11.	Aquarius the Water Bearer	.	.	.	.	♒
12.	Pisces the Fishes	.	.	.	.	♓

Now this division into twelve arises from the fact that the zodiac is constructed from the elements and qualities. Four signs belong to each of the three qualities, and one of each group of four belongs to each element. Thus:

	FIRE	WATER	AIR	EARTH
Cardinal . . .	Aries	Cancer	Libra	Capricorn
Fixed . . .	Leo	Scorpio	Aquarius	Taurus
Mutable . . .	Sagittarius	Pisces	Gemini	Virgo

The significance of the elements and qualities is explained in Chapter Four.

Further, all odd signs (i.e., fire and air) are called *Positive*, and all even signs (earth and water) are called *Negative*.

The positive signs are related to the masculine, outgoing, or aggressive side of Nature; the negative to the feminine, indrawn, or protective side. The former express themselves fully and freely on whatever line may be theirs; the latter are in principle reserved and receptive.

Sign-Rulership

The planets and signs are related by what is known as sign-rulership, each planet ruling two signs, called by some astrologers its "houses", although this term is ambiguous, since the word "house" has a special and altogether different meaning in Astrology, and it is equally easy to speak of a planet's sign, which is not open to misunderstanding. The Sun rules a positive and the Moon a negative sign, and each planet rules one of each.

This allocation of rulership is not arbitrary, as we shall see if we arrange the signs in two columns in their natural order, beginning with Leo at the head of the left-hand column, and travelling down that column and then up the next, so as to end with Cancer. We see that the signs then appear in pairs, each pair being ruled by one planet, while the planets are in the order of their distance from the Sun. Thus:

Leo	Cancer	ruled by Sun and Moon respectively.
Virgo	Gemini	ruled by Mercury.
Libra	Taurus	ruled by Venus.
Scorpio	Aries	ruled by Mars.
Sagittarius	Pisces	ruled by Jupiter.
Capricorn	Aquarius	ruled by Saturn.

Uranus, Neptune and Pluto have no definite rulerships, although they may have a special affinity, respectively, with Aquarius, Pisces and Scorpio.

Each body (excepting the three last-mentioned planets) has an *Exaltation*, or sign in which it is said to be particularly strong and favourable. These are:

Sun	.	. Aries	*Moon*	.	. Taurus
Mercury	.	. Virgo	*Venus*	.	. Pisces
Mars	.	. Capricorn	*Jupiter*	.	. Cancer
Saturn	.	. Libra			

The signs opposite its own signs are called the *detriments* of a planet, and the sign opposite its exaltation is called its *fall*. In its detriment or fall it is said to be weak.

Two bodies each in the sign of the others are said to be in *mutual reception*, which is considered to be harmonious. The *dispositor* of a planet is the ruler of the sign in which it is placed. Thus bodies in Aries or Scorpio are *disposed of* by Mars.

A body well placed (i.e., in its own sign or exaltation) is said to be *dignified*, but when the reverse is the case it is said to be *debilitated*.

These distinctions (and others now obsolete) have come down to us from ancient times and must not be taken too rigidly.

The Ruler or Lord of the Horoscope

It is considered that one body (Sun, Moon or planet) stands in a special sense in the nativity for the *native* or person for whom that nativity is erected, while the rest of the figure represents aspects of his life which are, relatively speaking, external to him, as for example, his friends, occupation, wife, children, and so on.

This body is called the Ruler or Lord of the Horoscope, and it is to it that astrologers refer when they call a person a "Martian" or "Uranian", or otherwise as the case may be.[1] It is usually the ruler of the 1st house,[2] but probably not invariably so, for if that body is very weak, whereas another is much stronger, as by rising near the ascendant,[2] with strong aspects (especially to the Sun, Moon or Mercury), or by being on the M.C., it may apparently become the ruler. It is then the representative of the personal self, much as the ascendant[2] and 1st house[2] generally are, and in a certain sense all the rest of the map may be regarded as external to it. Thus, if Mars afflicts the ruler we regard this as indicating that Martian matters are inimical to the native, and so on.

But in a deeper sense the entire nativity represents the native.

The signs start from the vernal equinox, or 0° Aries, which is the point in the zodiac at which the Sun, on about the 21st of March in each year, crosses the celestial equator and passes into north declination.

---

[1] When we speak of a person by the name of a sign, as an Arietic person, a Leo, and so on, we refer (or ought to refer) to the *rising sign*.

[2] To be explained in Section 4.

We may now explain four terms which even those who have made some progress in astrological studies do not always clearly understand.

Celestial Latitude[1] is the distance of a body north or south from the centre line of the zodiac. If we liken the zodiac to a path along which the planets travel, the line down the centre of that path is the *Ecliptic*, and all deviation north or south of this is latitude.

Celestial Longitude[2] is simply the distance of a body from 0° Aries, the beginning of the zodiac, stated in degrees and minutes (1 minute $= \frac{1}{60}$ of a degree) of the signs. This is the usual manner of describing the position of a planet. We say, for example, that a body is in the first degree of Gemini, meaning it is two signs, or 60 degrees, from 0° Aries.

Latitude and Longitude thus enable us to define the position in the sky of a body by measuring along the ecliptic and up and down from it.

We now come to two analogous measures related to the celestial equator, which is a projection of the earth's equator on to the heavens.

Right Ascension is measured along the equator from 0° Aries.

Declination is measured up and down (north and south) from the equator.

By this measure we define any point in the sky in relation to the celestial equator.

Longitude and Declination are the two most important measures from the standpoint of Astrology. Right Ascension and latitude are used in connection with certain kinds of prognostic work.

Other divisions of the signs besides that into degrees are employed astrologically, of which the one most frequently mentioned is that into thirds, of 10° each, called *Decans* or *Decanates*.

According to the Hindu system the first decanate of each sign is of the nature of that sign in its purity; the second decanate has a sub-influence of the next sign of the same element, and the last decanate a sub-influence of the last sign of that element.

For example:

0°–10° ♈ has a sub-influence of ♈;

10°–20° ♈ has a sub-influence of ♌;

20°–30° ♈ has a sub-influence of ♐ .

The so-called Chaldean system makes Mars the ruler of the first decanate of Aries and then allocates the decanates under the ancient bodies (omitting Uranus, Neptune and Pluto) in the reverse order of their apparent motion.

[1] Termed *Celestial* latitude in contradistinction to geographical.

[2] Termed *Celestial* longitude in contradistinction to geographical.

Thus the 2nd decanate of Aries is under the Sun, the 3rd under Venus; the 1st decanate of Taurus, under Mercury, the 2nd under the Moon, after which comes Saturn, then Jupiter ruling the 1st decanate of Gemini, and so on.

The beginner should thoroughly master the primary characteristics of the signs before troubling about the secondary.

The signs of the zodiac are not the same as the *Constellations* (groups of fixed stars) that bear the same names. At one time they were coincident, but, owing to what is called the precession of the equinoxes, this is no longer the case, so that, for example, the two well-known stars of the *constellation* Gemini, Castor and Pollux, are in the *sign* Cancer. The supposed ignorance of astrologers concerning the phenomenon of precession is often attacked by astronomers, though it is difficult to see upon what grounds, other than complete ignorance of astrological doctrine. In Western astrology the zodiac of constellations is but little employed. However, when reference is made to the so-called "Aquarian (or other) Age", it is the constellation Aquarius (or as the case may be) that is in question.

§ 4. THE HOUSES OF THE HOROSCOPE

These result from a division into twelve of the visible and invisible sky at any place and time. The sky above the horizon is divided into six sections, and similarly the sky beneath the horizon. These twelve sections are the familiar divisions of the horoscopical figure.

This division of the sky cuts the zodiac into twelve sections, which are not necessarily coincident with the twelve signs, and indeed in these latitudes never are. It is as if one watched a moving roadway through a window divided into six sections by fixed iron bars. The moving roadway might be itself divided into twelve sections (i.e., "signs"), but, as it moved, the bars of the window would cut it into sections that would rarely coincide with the divisions of the roadway itself.

Moreover, the twelve houses as usually determined do not (except at the equator) contain exactly 30° each, but vary in this respect, as we shall see later.

We, so to speak, watch the moving sky, which contains the

zodiac and planets, through the bars of the houses, which remain immovable, while the sky appears to sweep from east to west.

And while the sky sweeps round *from east to west* once in every twenty-four hours, this movement being caused by the rotation of the Earth on its axis, the sun, moon, and planets, owing to their real motion round the sun, gradually move *from west to east* through the signs of the zodiac.

The beginner must get a clear idea of the distinction between the signs, which are, so to speak, part of the sky itself and move with it, although invisible, and the houses, which as explained are, from the standpoint of the observer, stationary.

The houses are not named, but are known by their numbers, beginning with the 1st, immediately below the eastern horizon, and then following round as shown in the diagram on page 25.

The *cusp* of a house is its beginning, the dividing line between it and the preceding house. These are the "spokes" of the horoscopical wheel shown on page 25.

The cusp of the 1st house, on the eastern horizon, is called the *Ascendant* (abbreviation Asc.), and the cusp of the 10th (except in the "Equal House" System explained later) is called the *Midheaven* or M.C. (from Latin, *medium cœli*). The cusp of the 7th is sometimes called the *descendant*, and the cusp of the 4th the I.C. (from Latin, *imum cœli*).

Note that the terms zenith and nadir are sometimes incorrectly used for the M.C. and I.C. The zenith is the point directly over the observer's head and the nadir that immediately beneath his feet. They are at the intersections of the prime vertical and meridian.

The student must beware of thinking that the ascendant is *due* east. It is so only when 0° Aries or 0° Libra rises.

The 1st, 4th, 7th, and 10th houses, corresponding to the cardinal signs, are called *angular*.

The 2nd, 5th, 8th, and 11th, corresponding to the fixed signs, are called *succedent*.

The 3rd, 6th, 9th, and 12th, corresponding to the mutables, are called *cadent*.

Logically, however, there is no reason why new names should be used, for the houses correspond in nature to their respective signs. They are not classified according to element at all, but in this respect also there is no reason why the 1st, 5th, and 9th, for example, should not be called "fiery" houses, corresponding as they do to the fiery signs.

In a general sense the signs are said to relate to character, the houses to environment. Thus, Taurus (the 2nd *sign*) gives a love of comfort; the 2nd *house*, ruling possessions, bestows the means of gratifying it. In actual practice there seems little difference between a sign-position and the corresponding house-position so far as their relation to character and environment are concerned.

The houses are said to be *ruled* by the planet which rules the sign on its cusp, or, if a sign is intercepted,[1] its ruler is *part-ruler* of the house. This is styled *accidental rulership*, because it varies with each horoscope. The planet ruling the sign corresponding to a house is called the *essential* or *natural ruler* of that house. Thus, Venus is essential ruler of the 2nd and 7th, because it rules the 2nd and 7th signs; but any planet may be their accidental ruler.

The student should now study the diagram or horoscopic form shown on the following page.

A horoscope is a diagram of the heavens erected for any time and place for the purpose of astrological study. A horoscope for a birth-time is called a nativity, natus or geniture.

Horoscopes embody the three categories with which we have dealt, viz., the Sun, Moon, and Planets, the Signs, and the Houses.

The form below is not filled in; it merely gives the houses.

If the student wishes, he can cut out two forms similar to this,

1 See page 40.

using one (preferably transparent) to represent the houses, and the other the signs, the symbols of which he would then insert in place of the numbers of the houses in the first one. He can then pin the "houses" on to the "signs" and, keeping the first fixed, can revolve the other beneath it in the same direction as that traversed by the hands of a clock. It can then be clearly seen how the signs sweep through the houses, so that at one time Aries may be "rising", i.e., occupying the asc. or cusp of the 1st house, and afterwards Taurus, and so on.

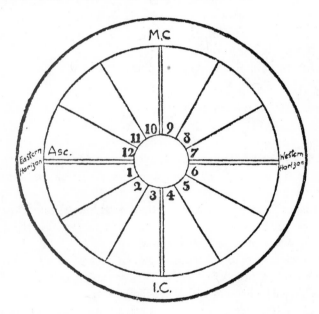

Furthermore, the planets may be inserted on the "signs" diagram, each in its own sign and degree, and they will then be carried round with the signs; but to complete the model it would be necessary for them to move slightly (about one degree a day in the case of the Sun) in an anti-clockwise direction through the degrees of the signs, this being their proper motion.

Those to whom the astronomical facts on which Astrology rests are not too clear may find some such model as this useful at this stage.

§ 5. THE ASPECTS

The Sun, Moon, and Planets are said to be *in aspect* with one another when placed at definite distances from each other in the zodiac, such distances, or aspects, being measured in degrees.

By dividing the 360° of the zodiac by 2, 4 and 8, we obtain the so-called *malefic* aspects which indicate opposing or inharmonious influences. By dividing it by 3, 6 and 12, we obtain the *benefic* or harmonious aspects.

The traditional aspects and their symbols are as follows:

	Good	Evil
Powerful	Trine, 120° △	Opposition, 180° ☌
	Sextile, 60° ✶	Square, 90° □
Weak	Semi-sextile, 30° ⅴ	Semi-square, 45° ∠
		Sesquiquadrate, 135° ⟗
		Quincunx, 150° ⚻

By some the opposition is regarded as not necessarily evil, but as indicating two complementary forces that can be harmonized.

It is more in accord with modern astrological thought to call the "good" aspects *facilitative* or *harmonizing* and the "bad" ones *obstructive* or *disruptive*.

The circle of 360° may also be divided by five, which produces the Quintile of 72° and its derivatives, i.e., the Vigintile of 18°, the Decile of 36°, the Tredecile of 108° and the Biquintile of 144°. All these are regarded as weak but benefic; the quintile, tredecile and biquintile being the most important.

The beginner should familiarize himself first with the trine, sextile, opposition and square, as also with:—

The Conjunction (symbol ☌) which occurs when two bodies are close together in the same sign, or at the end of one sign and beginning of the next.

This is the most powerful of all aspects, the opposition coming next, then the square, then the trine. The sextile may perhaps be equated with the semi-square and sesquiquadrate. There is little distinction to be made, in regard to strength or intensity, between the remainder.

The *Parallel of Declination* occurs when two bodies have the same declination or distance from the celestial equator. Whether both of them are north, both south, or one north and one south, appears immaterial. It is abbreviated as par. dec., par., or simply P.

These two last are good when formed between two benefics, or a benefic and a neutral, and doubtful when formed between benefics and malefics, the former being injured and the latter benefited in such a case. Between malefics and neutrals they are bad, although the student must in such cases pay attention to their respective natures, the sign occupied and other modifying factors. For instance, Sun conjunction Mars is far better than Moon conjunction the same planet, for the Sun is exalted in Aries, the sign of Mars, and so has affinity with the planet, but the Moon is in its fall in Scorpio, the other Martian sign, and so is uncongenial to the planet.

Two malefics in conjunction denote a critical feature in the life and character, and need careful study.

Special consideration should be given to the quadruplicity in which squares and oppositions fall.

Those in cardinal signs are apt to cause abrupt and sometimes complete changes in the activities and ways of thought.

Those in fixed signs appear often to lie dormant for long periods, though they may act drastically when they do act. In some respects they seem the least difficult of the three classes.

Those in mutable signs denote vacillation and indecision, the health is frequently seriously affected and accidents may occur. They appear to be the most troublesome of the three classes.

Orbs.—It rarely happens that an aspect is exact, that is, that any two bodies are *exactly* in square or trine, or any other aspect. The nearer they are to exactitude the stronger the aspect, but a certain sphere of influence is allowed to each body, called its orb.

Thus, if the Sun were in 0° ♈ and Mars in 0° ♌, they would be 120° apart, and therefore in exact trine. But if they were in 5° ♈ and 10° ♌ respectively, i.e., 125° apart, they would still be considered in trine, because of the orb allowable.

It may be said that for a ☌ or ☍ 9° may be allowed; for a △ or □ about 8°; for a ✳, about 7°; for the ∠ and ⊓, about 4°; for a ⦣, a parallel, a ⊼, or a quintile and its cognates, about 1°. A little more may be allowed for the Sun and Moon. For the Asc. or M.C., take about 5° as the maximum.[1]

Aspects are ordinarily formed from signs which are themselves in aspect. Thus a body in the beginning of Cancer is in square to one at the beginning of Libra and in trine to one at the beginning of Scorpio. But it would also be in trine to one at the *end* of Libra, although Libra is in square with Cancer. Such aspects are termed *dissociate*, and are often overlooked by beginners. It is probable that they are less powerful than those formed from the correct signs. Aspects may be *applying* or *separating*, according to whether the swifter of the two bodies involved is approaching or leaving exactitude. For example, Moon in 0° ♈ trine Sun in 5° ♌ is approaching, but Moon in 5° ♈ trine Sun in 0° ♌ would be separating. It is usually considered that, other things being equal, an applying contact is the more powerful.

The beginner should learn to reckon aspects not by counting from sign to sign, but by noting the signs containing the two bodies he is considering. All signs of the same quality are in square; all of the same element, in trine. Hence bodies in them,

---

[1] These are the orbs usually allowed. There is some tendency in modern times to lessen them.

if near the same degrees respectively, must also be in the same aspect.

Those who find it easier to reckon by rule of thumb may judge aspects as follows:

Start from the planet that is nearer 0° ♈ and count the signs forward to the sign containing the second body. For each sign take 30°. Thus, if the first planet is in Aries and the second in Virgo we should count five signs—♉, ♊, ♋, ♌, and ♍, which would equal 150° (5 × 30° = 150°).

Then add the degrees and minutes of the second body to this figure. For example, if it were in 5°31′ ♍ we should get 155°31′.

From this subtract the degrees and minutes of the first body. Thus, if this were in 18°24′ ♈ we should say

$$155°31′$$
$$Less \qquad 18°24′$$
$$\overline{137°07′}$$

Looking at the table we should find that this is near the sesquiquadrate (135°) and would in fact be within orbs of that aspect, for which we allow, as stated previously, 4°.

A Note on Aspects

Beginners should beware of an automatic classification of aspects into "good" and "bad" without due reference to the more general features of each figure, and, in particular, to the signs and houses occupied by the contacting bodies. This error is common even among comparatively experienced students. The so-called bad aspects are stronger than the good ones, and therefore are potentially more difficult, especially if the more vigorous planets are involved. But, on the other hand, it is quite arguable that, in the case of the less energetic bodies, a square is better than a trine, even if it may not be so "lucky".

A careful tabulation of many cases of good aspects on the one hand and bad aspects on the other, between the same bodies, has convinced the present writer that there is not always much to choose between them, heretical though this statement unquestionably is.

Undoubtedly the trine and sextile are harmonious contacts. But the maintenance of harmony is not the supreme end of human life, even though without some measure of harmonious adaptation, life would be impossible.

§ 6. MINOR CONSIDERATIONS[1]

Mundane Aspects

These are similar to the foregoing except that they are calculated in terms of *houses*, instead of *signs*. Thus, a planet on the cusp of the 4th would always be square one rising *mundanely*, although not necessarily zodiacally. Often bodies are in good aspect zodiacally and evil aspect mundanely, except on the equator, where they would always coincide. Their use introduces much difficulty in practical judgment; and although there is some evidence for their efficacy few students appear to employ them consistently, and the beginner should omit them.

The word "mundane" is often used in Astrology to denote something that has to do with the houses rather than the signs; indeed, it is often used as the adjective corresponding to the substantive "house", for which no recognized adjective exists, although some writers use "domal" in this sense, from the Latin *domus*.

The Part of Fortune

At this point mention must be made of what is called the Part of Fortune (symbolized ⊕).

This is a point in the horoscope which is at the same distance from the ascending degree, in either direction, as the Moon is from the Sun. In other words, it is to the asc. as the Moon is to the Sun. If the Sun and Moon are in conjunction, it will be conjunction with the asc.; if they are in opposition, it will be on the cusp of the 7th house, and so on.

It was believed by old writers, and some moderns, to affect the financial conditions of the native very powerfully. Others have doubted this, and some deny its influence entirely.

The present writer considers that it marks an important centre of interest in the native's life, and, if strong, shows success and honour, and the contrary if weak. But it is very questionable if its action is specifically financial. Thus, in the 3rd house it might show interest in writings and books, but not necessarily gain through literature. If badly afflicted it certainly seems to check the native's general success, as well as affecting the special matters denoted by its house.

Other "Parts" are sometimes used for the planets, all reckoned from the asc. and based on the distance or "elongation" of the planet from the Sun. Other sensitive points or parts are calculated by special rules left to us by seventeenth-century writers such as Gadbury, but none of these merits mention in an introductory work.

The Nodes

The Nodes of the Moon are the points in the ecliptic where ☽ passes from south to north latitude, and the reverse. The Ascending node is called the *Dragon's Head* (symbol ☊) and the Descending node the *Dragon's Tail*

[1] These may be omitted at the first reading.

(symbol ♉) and they are said to be of the natures, respectively, of Jupiter and Saturn, conferring honour and success or downfall and ruin. They are held to operate only by conjunction. Some writers deny or question their value. Others attach much importance to them, and also recommend using the planetary nodes.

Beginners are advised to defer such investigations to a later stage.

The Grand Trine

It sometimes happens that two bodies are in trine and a third body is in trine with each. Such a configuration was considered evil by medieval writers and unfortunately this view appears to be not without foundation. Often the fortunes seem to be greatly involved in those of others, both for good and evil, and the character may tend to weakness and lack of moral fibre. The element in which the grand trine falls may be too prominent in the temperament.

We have now completed our survey of all the main objects of astrological study, without, however, entering into the special powers or values of these objects. The beginner is advised thoroughly to master this chapter, including the symbols, the use of which is not only highly convenient, but absolutely essential, inasmuch as they are employed universally in astrological writings. Subsequent chapters, except perhaps the next, which deals with the erection of the horoscope, will be found much easier, involving as they do less memorization.

If not already acquainted with elementary astronomy, the student would be well advised to read a suitable book on this subject. The astronomical information given in such a standard work as *Whitaker's Almanack* is useful.

CHAPTER TWO

THE ERECTION OF THE HOROSCOPE

FOR this purpose we require the place, date, and time of birth (birth-data), and ephemeris (plural, ephemerides) or table of planetary positions, a table of houses for the approximate latitude of the place of birth, and, lastly, a horoscopic form or diagram.

The erection of the map involves two operations: calculating the *sidereal time of birth or right ascension of the mid-heaven* (*R.A.M.C.*) from which to obtain the *houses*, and then obtaining the *places of the planets* and inserting them in the houses.

Since figures bewilder many people who are in other respects likely to become good astrologers, we shall proceed from very simple cases to those which are somewhat more complicated.

As the great majority of our readers will be British, or will at least use an ephemeris calculated for Greenwich Mean Time (G.M.T.),[1] let us begin with a map for London, or, to be quite precise, for Greenwich.

Open the ephemeris for the year required at the month in question. Disregard the upper half of the two pages devoted to that month; they contain details not needed at this stage.

Find the day of the month by referring to the column on the left-hand side of the left page; the numbers therein are those of the days of the month. The next column shows the days of the week. The third column is headed Sidereal Time (abbreviated S.T.) and contains the sidereal time on the M.C. *at noon* at Greenwich for each successive day.

[1] Most ephemerides are calculated for noon at Greenwich, but the "American Astrology" ephemeris is based on 75° west longitude, the data being given for o hrs. Eastern Standard Time, which is five hours behind G.M.T.

Now copy down the S.T. for the *noon first preceding birth*.

If the birth-time is p.m. this will be noon of the same day; if it is a.m., it will be noon of the day before.

Now consider your given time of birth and ask: Is this given in G.M.T. or in summer time, or in double summer time?

THIS MUST ALWAYS BE THE FIRST QUESTION TO ASK.

British summer time was instituted in 1916 and the times of its beginning and ending, each year, are given in Whitaker's Almanack. When ordinary summer time is in operation, clocks are one hour in advance of G.M.T. During the war there was the additional complication of double summer time (2 hrs. instead of 1 hr.).

In some foreign countries all sorts of difficulties arise in regard to summer time; but these do not now concern us. It is, after all, the responsibility of the person who submits the data to the astrologer to clarify this point.

Now, having deducted one hour for ordinary summer time, or two for double summer time, or having decided that neither applies, take the S.T. at noon, which you have copied down, and add to it the interval of time between that noon and the moment of birth.

Thus, for example, you are told that a child was born at 2.30 p.m. on January 2, 1950, at Greenwich.

There was no summer time in operation and the previous S.T. at noon was 18 hrs. 46 m. 13 s.

hrs.	min.	sec.
18	46	13
2	30	0
21	16	13

But suppose it had been 2 hrs. 30 m. *a.m.*
You follow the same rule.

The previous noon will now be January 1, 1950, when the S.T. was 18 hrs. 42 m. 16 s.

Very well:

hrs.	min.	sec.
18	42	16
14	30	0
33	12	16

from which you must deduct 24 hrs. and thus get as answer:

9 hrs. 12 m. 16 s.

Whenever your result exceeds 24 hours take that time from it and the remainder is your answer.

Is the above quite right?

No, not quite. The reason for this is that the times of birth you have added are clock-time hours and minutes, whereas your answer must be in sidereal time, which is slightly different. To every 24 hours of clock or mean time, there are 24 hrs. 3 m. 56½ s. of sidereal time.

Therefore we get a correction to be applied to our 2 hrs. 30 m. and 14 hrs. 30 m., and this amounts to adding approximately ten seconds for each hour; to be precise, 9.86 seconds. Or say 10 secs. for every hour less one second for every minute of correction.

Therefore to 2 hrs. 30 m. we must add approximately twenty-five seconds, and to 14 hrs. 30 m. we must add 2 m. 25 s., or, to be exact, 2 m. 23 s.

It is obvious that unless the time of birth is known almost precisely, this correction is a waste of time, but it is necessary to employ it in some kinds of astrological work, and the student must form the habit of using it.

We have now dealt with all maps for the longitude of Greenwich, whatever their latitude. For example, what has been written above will apply equally for births at Boston in Lincoln-shire or Seaford in Sussex.

Let us now deal with the question of *geographical latitude* once and for all.

This only enters into the matter in so far as we must use a table of houses for (approximately) the latitude of the place of birth; it does not affect the calculation of the S.T. of birth, which is concerned only with geographical *longitude*.

A table of houses calculated for a latitude of not more than half a degree from the latitude of the place of birth would be considered near enough for ordinary purposes.

Now supposing our place of birth is somewhere using G.M.T. as its standard of clock time, but with a longitude east or west of Greenwich, say Paris or Bath.

The rule here is very simple:

Add four minutes to your result, obtained as above, for every degree of east longitude, and *subtract* four minutes for every degree of west longitude.

Thus for Paris you will add 9 m. 20 s. (2° 20′ east) and for Bath you will subtract 9 m. 24 s. (2° 21′ west).

Special Note: Always state clearly and carefully upon your maps the nature of the time in which the data are recorded, whether G.M.T., Central European, and so forth, and whether summer time is involved.

We come now to those maps which most beginners regard with apprehension, quite unnecessarily.

These are maps based on standard times other than that of Greenwich.

The rule here is really very simple.

Find the sidereal time at Greenwich[1] when the birth actually took place.

[1]Actually reduce to the standard time upon which your ephemeris is based. See note above on "American Astrology" ephemeris.

Suppose, for example, it was at Cologne at 3 p.m., local standard time, which is 1 hour fast of Greenwich. Then the G.M.T. at that moment was 2 p.m. So find the S.T. at Greenwich at 2 p.m.

Let us take January 1, 1950.

				hrs.	min.	sec.
Noon S.T.	.	.	.	18	42	16
Add	.	.	.	2	0	0
Correction	.	.	.			20
				20	42	36

Now find the longitude of Cologne. It is 6° 57′ east.

Convert this into time by multiplying it by 4 and calling minutes of longitude seconds of time, and degrees of longitude minutes of time. The result will be 27 m. 48 s.

Since this is east, you will add it to the above result and obtain 21 hrs. 10 m. 24 s.

Erect the map for this sidereal time. Tables for Taunton (if you have the "Table of Houses for the British Isles" booklet) will be sufficiently near for all ordinary purposes.

Note that the correction of 20 seconds is applied *after* you have reduced the local standard time (in this case Central European) to Greenwich. That is to say, it is applied to 2 hours, not 3 hours.

Thus easily you can obtain the S.T. of birth for any place on the globe that employs a standard time.

It is very unlikely that you will ever meet a case wherein you are told that there is no standard time in use, but, in such an event, the data may be either true solar time (i.e., what the sundial would record) or local mean time. In both cases it would be necessary for you to convert the given time into the standard time for which your ephemeris is calculated, and then proceed in the manner already described.

Mean or clock time is a convention adopted to maintain a constant length of day throughout the year, and consequently it does not always coincide with true solar time. Owing to slight variations which occur in the Sun's apparent daily rate of motion, mean time is sometimes ahead of true solar time and sometimes behind it. The difference is known as the "equation of time", and may be as much as 16 m. 24 s. It is tabulated daily in *Whitaker's Almanack* and in *American Astrology* Ephemeris.

If you should ever be given the hour of birth in "apparent" or true solar time (the hour either having been taken from a sundial or by direct solar observation), it can readily be turned into local mean time by applying the equation of time.

The local mean time so found would be the clock time *for that particular longitude*, and to convert it into the standard time of the ephemeris you must first find the difference in longitude between that place and that on which the ephemeris is based. Allowing four minutes of time for a degree as before, the difference should be *subtracted* from the local mean time if the place is east of the ephemeristic meridian, and *added* if west. Having thus obtained the birth hour in terms of the standard time for which the ephemeris is computed, you proceed as before.

It may seem rather silly to subtract from the local mean time an amount equivalent to the difference in longitude to obtain the ephemeristic standard, only to add the same difference to the result in the manner already described, but there is a very good reason for this. By following the various steps in their proper order a further correction in the sidereal time covering the difference in longitude is accounted for without introducing further complications, and in any case the standard time of the ephemeris must be used when calculating the planetary positions (see below).

Let us recapitulate in four simple rules:—

1. Correct for Summer Time if necessary.

2. When using the ephemeris calculated for Greenwich mean noon, reduce the stated time of birth to G.M.T. by adding or subtracting the difference between the regional standard time and G.M.T.

3. From that G.M.T. find the corresponding S.T. (including the correction from clock time to sidereal time).

4. Add to, or subtract from, this the equivalent in time of the east or west longitude of the place of birth.

Some further examples:

Suppose the child had been born at Melbourne at 2.0 p.m., January 1, 1950. Melbourne standard time is 10 hours fast of Greenwich, so that it was 4 a.m. of the same day by G.M.T.

Proceed:

	hrs.	min.	sec.
Noon, December 31, 1949 .	18	38	20
Add	16	0	0
Add correction . . .		2	38
	34	40	58
Subtract	24	0	0
	10	40	58
For Melbourne, which is 145° 2' east, add . .	9	40	8
	20	21	6

In practice it is customary to omit seconds, except for special work, and to write the S.T. to the nearest minute.

Let us now take two U.S.A. examples, omitting seconds.

Child born at 2.0 p.m., January 1, 1950, at New York. Eastern Standard Time is 5 hours behind Greenwich, so that this is equivalent to 7 p.m. G.M.T.

	hrs.	min.
S.T. Noon	18	42
Add	7	0
Correction		1
	25	43
Less correction for longitude of New York	4	56
	20	47

Supposing we are using the "American Astrology" ephemeris which is calculated for Eastern Standard Time, the S.T. being given, not for noon, but for o hrs. o m. of each day, i.e., for midnight.

Then

	hrs.	min.
S.T. midnight, January 1, 1950.	6	41
Add for 2 p.m. . . .	14	0
Correction for 14 hours . .		2
Add (because New York is 1° east of the East Standard Time meridian)		4
	20	47

Other U.S.A. examples are given in the ephemeris itself.

Now having obtained your sidereal time of birth, turn to the table of houses for the latitude required, or as near thereto as you can find, and take the column headed "Sidereal Time". Beneath this heading you will see the hours, minutes and seconds of S.T., beginning at o hrs. o m. o s. (top left-hand corner of left-hand page).

In this column find the S.T. that you require (or as close as you can get) and opposite this you will find the degrees and signs that, at that time, at the latitude in question, occupy the 10th, 11th, 12th, 1st, 2nd, and 3rd cusps respectively, according to the system of house division for which the tables you are using are calculated.

Insert these signs and degrees in your diagram and opposite them the *same* degrees of the *opposite* signs. Thus if 17 ♏ is on cusp 2, then 17 ♉ will be on cusp 8, and so on.

You then have your houses completed.

But in inserting these data it must not surprise you if you

find (in these latitudes and still more in latitudes nearer the poles) that some signs are left out. For example, at London you will find that if Aquarius rises (i.e., is on cusp 1) then Aries is always on cusp 2, so that Pisces, the intervening sign, is not on any cusp at all.

Such signs are said to be *intercepted*.

In the so-called equal method of house division mentioned later interception cannot occur, nor does it happen near the equator by any recognized system.

Birth in Southern Latitudes

Here we have two simple additional adjustments.

Work exactly as before, but to your answer add 12 hours.

When you insert the degrees and signs on the spokes of the horoscopic figure, use the degrees given in the Table of Houses, but insert the *opposite* signs.

It will be seen that, in some circumstances, the erection of the houses is a matter calling for care, if not for actual skill. But by proceeding step by step, as explained previously, the possibility of error will be greatly reduced. *When you have finished your horoscope it is a good plan to glance at the position of the Sun, which must, of course, roughly indicate the time of birth. This serves as a check on any serious error.*

To Insert Planets: Birth in England or Scotland

Use the Greenwich time without any adjustment.

The planetary positions are given for noon, and, if the birth is at noon, are simply copied out.

If the birth is before or after noon it is necessary to find their daily motion (given in Raphael's ephemeris, but in any case easily found by subtraction), and then to work out a little sum to find how far they would go in a certain time (i.e., the time before or after noon at which birth took place) in view of the fact that they go so far in the day. With the slower-moving planets this can be seen at a glance, but with the others it must be worked out.

Suppose, for example, birth is at 3 p.m. January 2, 1930, and we want the position of Mars. We see that at noon he was in 3° 3′ ♑, and at noon on the next day at 3° 49′ ♑. Thus his daily motion = 46′. Then how far will he go in three hours? The answer is ⅛ of 46′, or about 6′, and we therefore add this to the noon position, and get 3° 9′ ♑. If birth were 9 a.m. we should, of course, *subtract* 6′ from the noon position.

The student is advised, however, to use the logarithmic method explained at the end of the ephemeris. Logarithms may sound difficult, but the reverse is the case, and their use practically makes error impossible. The method is explained and exemplified in the ephemeris, and therefore requires no treatment here.

To Insert Planets: Birth Abroad

The positions in the ephemeris are for noon at Greenwich, and therefore are only true as noon-positions for places using Greenwich time.

For all other places, the time in which birth is recorded (whether local or standard for the country) must be reduced to the corresponding Greenwich time, which has already been found, for which calculate the planetary positions from the ephemeris in the ordinary way.

This method applies equally to places south of the equator.

As an example take a birth at noon at New York. This time would be recorded in U.S.A. "Eastern Time" which is for 75° east. This equals 5 hours, and as it is west it must be added to the time to yield the Greenwich equivalent. Therefore, calculate the planets for 5 p.m.

Again, if birth were at Melbourne, Australia, at noon, we should have to subtract 10 hours and reckon the map for 2 a.m. Greenwich, because Melbourne uses a meridian of 150° east.

For many purposes it is sufficient to calculate planets and angles to the nearest degree or half-degree.

But if you do this do not insert the minutes; put the nearest degree and omit them altogether. To insert them would imply that they have been calculated. Thus, 11° 49′ ♒ may be written as 12 ♒; 7° 24′♉, as 7♉, or 7½♉.

Example.—Required a horoscope for 2 hrs. 44 m. p.m., January 1, 1924, at Sheffield.

We can for this purpose use Liverpool houses, the difference in latitude being slight. The longitude is about 1° 30′ west.

	hrs.	min.	sec.
S.T. Noon, January 1, 1924	18	39	30
Time of birth p.m. .	2	44	0
Correction . . .			27
	21	23	57
Correction for west longitude			6	0
	21	17	57

Turning to the tables of houses for Liverpool we find a S.T. of 21 hrs. 17 m. 49 s., which is very near, and is quite close enough for approximate work. We then copy out the degrees given in the table, making the asc. 26° ♊, for if it was 25° 30′ at S.T. 21 hrs. 17 m. 49 s., then at 21 hrs. 17 m. 57 s. it must be a little more, and therefore nearer 26° ♊ than 25° ♊. We should enter the M.C. as 17° ♊, but not as 17° 0′, because this would be incorrect. A little sum will show us that at 21 hrs. 17 m. 58 s. the ascendant is really 25° 32′ ♊ and the M.C. 17° 2′ ♒.

The cusps of the succedent and cadent houses are always taken to the nearest degree only.

To calculate the planets, we take the Greenwich time (since Sheffield uses this standard) without any correction, i.e., 2 hrs. 44 m. p.m.

The log. for this time is 0.9435.

Add this to the log. for the daily motion of each planet, and the result is the log. of the motion of that body in 2 hrs. 44 m. Since the birth was p.m. *add* this to the planets' noon-positions, and you obtain their places at birth.

Two examples should suffice:

Daily motion of Moon to nearest minute =	
14° 28′ =	0.2198
Add log. of 2 hrs. 44 m. =	0.9435
	1.1633

This is seen to equal 1° 39′. Add this to the Moon's noon-position, which is 0° 58′ ♏ and we have 2° 37′ ♏ as the ☽'s position at birth.

Now take Mars:

Daily motion of Mars between noon January 1 and noon January 2 is 39′ = log. 1.5673

Add log.   0.9435

2.5108 = 4′
(approximately)

4′ is then added to the noon-position, yielding 18° 19′ ♏.

It is easy roughly to check this result. 2 hrs. 44 m. is obviously somewhat less than one-eighth of the day of 24 hrs., therefore the result must be something less than one-eighth of 39′, which it is in fact seen to be.

Jupiter, Saturn, Uranus and Neptune move so slowly that it will not be worth while to calculate their positions by the foregoing method. For example, the daily motion of Jupiter at the above time is seen to be 12'; an eighth of this would be 1½', and as 2 hrs. 44 m. is less than one-eighth, Jupiter's motion will be less than 1½', that is, it will be stated, to the nearest minute, as 1'. Saturn's motion is 4', so that, in an eighth of the day, it would be ½', and as our time is less than one-eighth we should make no alteration to the noon-position at all, because his motion will be nearer nothing than 1'.

We now have our horoscope complete, as shown above.

An Important Note

We have explained above how the houses of the horoscope are calculated with the use of the tables of houses most in vogue. These are calculated according to the method of Placidus, which came into common use in Britain at the beginning of the nineteenth century. Previously another system, different in theory but productive of not very dissimilar results, was employed: this is named after its inventor, Regiomontanus. In modern times there is a tendency to revert to the simple Ptolemaic or "equal" method. In erecting a map by this system it is only necessary to find the ascendant in the manner already described (that is to say, from the tables of houses for the latitude in question) and then to add 30° for each cusp, so that, for example, if the ascendant be 5° Aries, the cusp of the 2nd house is 5° Taurus, and so on successively round the figure.

A further note on House-division (or Domification) is given later (pp. 88-91).

Further Considerations

Retrogression.—We have said that the planets' proper motion is in the order of the signs, that is to say, it is the reverse of that of the hands of the clock, whereas their apparent motion, due to the earth's rotation, is clockwise.

At times, however, they appear to slow down, remain stationary, and then reverse their proper motion. Then, after a while, they slow down again, remain stationary, and then resume their normal movement. The Sun and Moon are the only exceptions.

The reason for this is not hard to understand.

Imagine yourself walking in a circle round a central point, while another person does the same, in the same direction, but at a different distance, either greater or less than yours. A moment's reflection will show you that when he is on the same side of the centre as yourself he will seem to be going in one direction (if you watch him on the background of the various objects in the room, as we watch the planets on the background of the fixed stars), whilst when he is on the opposite side of the centre he will appear to be moving in the reverse direction.

Planets are therefore said to be *direct* when going in the sense of the zodiac, but *retrograde* (written ℞) when not doing so, and they can be *stationary to direct* or *stationary to retrograde*, and vice versa.

Retrograde motion is said to weaken planets, and to delay the fruits of their action, though it is debated whether these effects operate only in lessening and hindering benefic action, or whether evil action is also diminished, supposing they are in bad aspect.

The present writer has seen no real evidence whatever to lead him to suppose that, in natal astrology, retrogression has a baleful effect. On the contrary, since a retrograde planet moves clockwise in the ecliptic, i.e., from east to west, so that its zodiacal motion agrees with its diurnal motion, due to the earth's rotation, such a body may even be disposed to operate more constructively, other things being equal, than when it is direct.

Stationary planets are probably strong; they certainly are so in some circumstances (see Chapter on Prognostication).

Declinations.—These must be calculated from the ephemeris. The motion is so slow that the correct figures can usually be obtained in all cases (except that of the Moon) by mere inspection. The Moon can be worked in the same way as for longitude.

Tabulation of Aspects.—At first the beginner will find aspects difficult to detect, and he will probably attempt to find them by counting the signs intervening between the bodies, in which case he must beware of intercepted signs. Later he will learn to see aspects quite easily by observing the signs occupied by the bodies he is examining.

All signs of the same element are in trine, and all of the same quality in square. Fire and air signs are in sextile or opposition, and similarly water and earth.

The beginner may advantageously omit the minor aspects at first.

The aspects in the horoscope on page 44 may be tabulated as follows:

	☽	☿	♀	♂	♃	♄	♅	♆	Asc.	M.C.	Declination
☉	＊						＊				23.5 S.
☽		⬓	□			☌	⬓				4.46 N.
☿			*P*		*P*	□	∠				20.49 S.
♀					*P* ＊	□			⬓		20.0 S.
♂							△	□		□	16.36 S.
♃							□				21.0 S.
♄							⬓		△		9.33 S.
♅											6.54 S.
♆									＊	☍	15.4 N.

Note that in this form of tabulation each aspect is only entered once, and in order to see what aspect a body has it is necessary to go down the vertical line, headed by its symbol, until one reaches the horizontal line belonging to it, and then travel along that horizontal line. Thus, to find the aspects of Venus above, we begin with the vertical line, and see that it is □ ☽ and P ☿; then we run along the horizontal line, and find that it is ✶ and P ♃, □ ♄, ⊡ Asc.

Students should cultivate care and neatness in drawing up horoscopes. Proper forms can be bought cheaply, while a loose-leaf ledger or card-index system will appeal to those who aim at a really useful collection of nativities. A rubber stamp, in the usual horoscopic form, can be bought from a stationer's for a few shillings, and forms can then be printed *ad lib.* on cards, pages of books, etc. as may be desired.

Standard Times

Since these are subject to alteration, from time to time, in certain countries, it is advisable, when dealing with non-British data, to make direct inquiries as to this point.

CHAPTER THREE

THE SUN, MOON AND PLANETS IN DETAIL

§ 1. PLANETARY STRENGTH

THE Sun, Moon, and Planets are all present in every horoscope, and their action is to some extent felt in the life of everyone. But in this respect each nativity varies.

A planet may be strong or weak with regard to (*a*) sign-position, (*b*) house-position, and (*c*) aspects; that is to say, *zodiacally*, *mundanely*, or *by aspect*.

It is strong mundanely if it is angular, and weakest if it is cadent. It is always stronger when near the cusp of a house than when it is near the end, so that the very strongest places are the cusps of angles, especially the asc. and the M.C. But mundane strength has relation to prominence in the life, or, on the other hand, to obscurity, rather than goodness or badness of influence. Mars exactly rising will be very prominent in the life of the native, for example, but whether it has a good or an evil effect depends rather on sign and aspect. Similarly a planet at the end of the 6th house is not likely to figure prominently in the life, but such action as it has will be good or ill according to sign and aspect.

Angular positions favour manifestation in action; succedent work out largely through the feelings, and so may be repressed for long periods; cadent positions largely affect thought, and so may remain in the "subconscious" for years, although their influence is there all the time.

Thus, when it is said that a body is strongest when angular, this should be taken to mean that its value is then usually most obvious but not that it is necessarily more important, in a true sense, than when it is succedent or cadent. That would be a superficial view to adopt.

Zodiacal and aspectual strength decides whether the action of the planet will be harmonious and easy, or distorted, troublesome, and apt to lead one astray. A planet is strongest in its own signs, and, after that, in its exaltation, although it is thought by many that in the former case it is rendered more powerful, and in the latter actually manifests a finer and more desirable action. Thus it is found that Saturn in Capricorn is a very clearly marked and decided Saturnian influence, whereas Saturn in Libra is refined and rendered less austere.

Actually sign-position cannot be reduced to cut-and-dried rules; each must be specially studied. For example, in a general sense Mars is stronger in Aries than in Pisces, but from the standpoint of kindliness it would be much more favourably placed in the second.

The Ancients thought that a planet showed its best side in its positive sign and its worst in its negative; thus Mars was courageous in Aries, but treacherous in Scorpio, Saturn was grave and sober in Aquarius, but sour and melancholy in Capricorn. This is quite untrue.

We will now consider the typical action of the various bodies, beginning with those ruling fire and water signs, and then passing to those that rule earth and air, and ending with Uranus, Neptune and Pluto, whose rulerships (if any) are uncertain.

§ 2. The Sun ⊙

The Sun is the ruler of Leo, fixed fire, and is exalted in Aries. From it come all the positive powers of our nature, all those that urge us outward and forward, and make for strong and vigorous manifestation on the physical plane. A well-placed Sun makes for dignity, self-reliance, strength of character, just appreciation of one's value, abundant affections, and ready helpfulness, with powers of leadership, control, and command. There are virile animal spirits, buoyancy, magnanimity, and a large and open way of viewing and dealing with life.

If the Sun is obscurely placed these qualities are lacking.

A prominent but afflicted Sun (i.e., strong mundanely, but weak by sign and aspect) gives a semblance of the solar virtues, but they tend to run to excess and lack balance and common sense to control them; the native is apt to be ostentatious, bombastic, promising much and performing little, trying to lead, but often being, in fact, a puppet in the hands of favourites and sycophants. The affection may degenerate into sensuality, maudlin sentiment, or mere verbal affection, masking real selfishness. The self-confidence is either excessive or else hides inner cowardice and incompetence.

We get, in fact, many of the qualities that one associates with a bad monarch.

The action of the Sun, when strong, is fortifying and vitalizing in whatever part of the map it is placed.

§ 3. THE MOON ☽

As the Sun is the only body that exclusively represents fire, so, with the possible exception of Neptune, the Moon alone rules only water. It is the ruler of Cancer, cardinal water, and is exalted in Taurus.

As the Sun stands for the positive self-expressive part of our nature, so the Moon stands for the feminine, indrawn, receptive, and imaginative side. It tends towards carefulness, prudence, timidity, shyness, and the secluded domestic life, although the lunar person is often shrewd and practical in business. It is maternal, affectionate, sympathetic, impressionable, given to moods, easily roused emotionally, changeful, and yet tenacious and enduring in regard to its own activities, just as women, though reputedly changeable, are patient and enduring in those phases of life that are their special work, and are braver *passively* than men.

The lunar nature dwells much in the past and has a long memory. It is inclined to be clannish, prejudiced, and narrow in its sympathies, which are at first often limited to the home and family, but can expand so as to include wider and wider circles.

There is sometimes morbid sensitiveness and self-consciousness.

The action of the Moon may be described as fluctuating, variable, absorbent, and receptive.

§ 4. MARS ♂

This planet rules Aries, cardinal fire, and Scorpio, fixed water, and it is exalted in Capricorn. It is in its own nature fiery and in many respects resembles the Sun. Its action, however, is more energizing and less stable; it gives physical activity, enterprise, push, courage, and endurance, showing the more positive side through Aries and the more negative side through Scorpio. It bestows nerve, muscular power, and the ability to "rough it".

It is quick, decisive, restless, apt to do things single-handed, and "run the show", believing that no one else can do as well. It may be quarrelsome, reckless, self-opinionated, and excessive in words, feelings, and actions. In bad cases it may even give cruelty and brutality, and if prominent there is seldom great refinement, the tendency being to get on with things and not beat about the bush with what appear to it as needless courtesies.

There is a great dislike of interference and a love of freedom and personal liberty, which, in the case of an evolved Martian, may produce a valiant and idealistic fighter on behalf of the weak; this, indeed, is the highest type produced by Mars.

Its action is sudden, self-assertive, and disruptive.

§ 5. JUPITER ♃

Jupiter rules Sagittarius, mutable fire, and Pisces, mutable water. It is exalted in Cancer, in which sign it gains kindliness and gentleness, and expands the sympathies of the sign beyond the home-circle to which they are apt to be limited. The key-word of Jupiter is *expansion*.

Being an entirely mutable planet, its action is largely on the mental plane, and it makes the philosopher, scientist, theologian, and speculative thinker of all kinds. It has also great power in the moral and material worlds, making the nature kind, generous, hopeful, and loyal, while the fortunes are improved. Indeed, Jupiter, unless badly afflicted, is the planet of luck, i.e., of good fortune not clearly attributable to merit, and those with the planet angular and in a congenial sign are usually fortunate beyond the average, especially if they possess common sense and a sense of moderation; otherwise they tempt their fortunes too far. In some respects it resembles the Sun and Mars, though more mental, and under affliction it runs, like these bodies, to excess of energy, optimism, and self-indulgence. The faith becomes an unbounded belief in luck and a reckless disregard of consequences, so that, although seldom anyone's enemy but his own, the Jovian often ruins himself by pushing his luck too far, taking unreasonable hazards, gambling, and wasting time, money, and energy.

Jupiter has much to do with sports, hunting, athletics, and also with fondness for animals.

An obscure Jupiter may denote a mean, joyless, pessimistic nature.

The action of the planet, when well placed, is that of orderly and healthy growth or increase.

It will be seen that the three fire bodies closely resemble one another. They all make for exuberance of life and self-expression, inclining to the aggressive and self-assertive. Under affliction they may be noisy, loud, quarrelsome, or vain, according to the special features of each case. When their influence is lacking, the native tends to have no warmth of nature, and to be spiritless, without ideals or enthusiasms, timid, unsocial, or humdrum.

We now come to three bodies, each of which rules one earth and one air sign. They operate chiefly mentally, the airy side being more akin to abstract thought, and the earthy to that which is concrete and tangible.

§ 6. VENUS ♀

This planet rules Libra, cardinal air, and Taurus, fixed earth. It is exalted in Pisces, wherein its sympathies expand; it loses its ultra-refinement and tendency to dislike "soiling its hands" with the affairs of its less fortunate brethren.

Venus is the planet of harmony, or *adaptation*, the highest expression of which, emotionally, is love.[1] The Venusian love is understanding, idealistic, and universal, while that of Leo is usually warmer and more passional.

Every work that requires collaboration, unification, co-operation, and the joining of hands for a common purpose is under the influence of this planet, which enables people to see common interests where Mars causes them to see points of difference.

When strong it gives a well-balanced, impartial, fair, placid disposition, refined, and devoted to the arts, fond of social pleasures, often lovable, but, of itself, unfitted for arduous or disagreeable work. It may be said that as a good Jupiter gives prosperity, so Venus gives happiness, by harmonizing the emotions.

A prominent but afflicted Venus gives laziness, dependence on others, carelessness, lack of enterprise and confidence, a

---

[1] Sexual love, or desire, is a ☉ ♂ activity; from this point of view ♀ is rather the beloved.

parasitic attitude, day-dreaming, and unpracticality. The attractions bestowed by the planet may be used meretriciously to secure advantages.

A Venus obscurely placed in the horoscope is apt to denote the native to be boorish and uncultured.

The action of the planet is gentle and harmonious, but not very strong as regards things of the physical world.

§ 7. MERCURY ☿

This planet rules Gemini, mutable air, and Virgo, mutable earth, and is said to be exalted in its own sign, Virgo. By some it is considered exalted in Aquarius, where it becomes steadied and humanized.

The basic conception of Mercury is *intercommunication.* Hence its rule over thought and speech and writing, especially the writing of letters; for the same reason, it rules short journeys and all that ministers to them, such as the roads, bicycles, trams, and buses. It rules trade, which is the exchange of commodities, and is one of the planets most valuable in business. When prominent, it gives a quick, inquiring mind and ready expression with tongue and pen. There is a strong sense of logic, and a rapid comprehension of facts, often with a taste for detail rather than generalities. It may be a brilliant talker, and often possesses encyclopaedic knowledge. Note that it is not imaginative. Imagination is rather lunar and Neptunian. It is exact, matter-of-fact, and critical.

Under affliction, the mental powers are seldom lessened, but their expression may be vitiated by a tendency to untruthfulness, exaggeration, sarcasm, or ill-temper, according to the nature of the affliction. There may be a liking for hair-splitting or quibbling, too great immersion in detail, or even a criminal misapplication of the mental powers, as in slander, libel, defalcation, or theft.

An obscure Mercury spoils the mental abilitities, or at least prevents the native from expressing them easily.

The action of the planet is quick, volatile, and uncertain.

§ 8. SATURN ♄

This body rules Aquarius, fixed air, and Capricorn, cardinal earth. It is exalted in Libra, wherein it becomes gentler and more merciful, for of itself Saturn is the planet of strict justice that demands full payment for all that it bestows. It is *the planet of the concrete and practical*, and gives a vivid sense of material values and what are called hard facts. When strong it gives most of the virtues of what may be called the "self-help" type, such as patience, perseverance, hard work, thrift, concentration, solidity, and reliability.

It is the planet of *limitation*, and even when well placed in the horoscope the native who comes much under its ray is apt to be limited and circumscribed in his views and sympathies, conservative, cautious, and narrow.

When ill-placed as regards sign and aspect, but prominent by house, it is apt to show meanness, selfishness, a sense of heavy responsibilities, and a despondent, sad outlook. In this respect it may be contrasted with the three fiery planets and their typical optimism and faith—in God, luck, or themselves, according to their stage in moral evolution. The true Saturnian usually believes that nothing can be won without hard work, and he has both the virtues and the vices of this belief. It is the planet of real worth, as apart from show and make-believe, and gives to all things their permanent and lasting qualities. On the other hand, by limiting the outgoing activities of fire, it causes checks, delays, and disappointments, and so becomes the planet of fate, which sets definite bounds to our efforts.

Its action is slow, thorough, and inevitable.

§ 9. Uranus ♅

This planet is said by some to rule Aquarius and by others is connected with Scorpio, but in the writer's opinion it is doubtful if it rules these or any other signs, although it has more affinity with them than with the others. It has the energy of fire, the emotional nature of water, and the intellect of air, and is perhaps least allied to earth.

It bestows originality, versatility, ability of many kinds, and good intellectual powers, so that it combines something of Mars and Mercury, but in pursuit of a chosen end it will manifest the virtues of Saturn as well, and display patience, organizing powers, and hard common sense. It is also in some respects like the Sun, for it tends to seek out positions of power and responsibility, and abhors limitation or restriction.

It has much to do with administration and on its more normal or conventional side it appears to rule both local and national government, official appointments and officialdom generally and those holding positions of authority and control.

When rising it gives an unconventional but good-natured type, outspoken, forthright and rough-and-ready.

Under affliction it easily manifests eccentricity and produces a gifted but useless crank, always at loggerheads with custom, irrespective of whether this is supported by common sense or not, so that it spends its time and energies fighting needless battles with convention and authority. It may also display moodiness, morbid sensitiveness, and a particularly explosive and at the same time unforgetting temper, with bitter resentments of fancied slights and injuries, in this respect recalling the worse side of Scorpio. It is, therefore, a critical influence; and while it may bestow unique powers, it may also produce very undependable and even dangerous characters.

Persons with Uranus prominent tend to have a peculiar nervous constitution.

Its weakness in a map shows lack of originality and independence.

It is claimed as peculiarly the astrological planet.

The action of Uranus is sudden, unexpected, and drastic.

§ 10. Neptune Ψ

This planet, like Uranus, was discovered in modern times and has no recognized sign-rulership, but experience connects it with Pisces.

As Uranus resembles in some respects the Sun, Mercury, Mars, and Saturn, so Neptune has a delicate musical and artistic sense and an idealism and spirituality that recall Venus, whilst in other ways it is reminiscent of Jupiter, and its connection with drugs and poisons is distinctly Piscean.

It has a clear connection with all maritime matters, and indeed with many things related to liquidity.

It is the planet of the creative imagination, ranging downwards from the inspirations of the great poets and artists to the terrible and diseased fancies of the criminal and mentally afflicted. It is the planet of pretence and deception, including self-deception; it has a general tendency to make things appear other than they are, whence its relation to the stage and the films. Those with a badly placed Neptune cannot be too careful to exercise common sense and to avoid all that is not entirely aboveboard, plain, and straightforward, and they should never place their affairs in the hands of any but firms of the highest standing. Otherwise they will find themselves involved in muddle, if not in actually dangerous circumstances.

Neptune appears to rule spiritualism and kindred practices.

It is extremely sensitive, both physically and mentally; hence the tendency to worry. In fact Neptune often causes worry rather than actual misfortune. It is less definitely privative than Saturn, yet it often calls for the exercise of renunciation.

Its best values are spiritual; in worldly matters its good effects are often imposing rather than substantial.

The action of Neptune is subtle, gradual, and sometimes insidious.

§ 11. PLUTO (Symbol not yet determined)

This body was discovered in the early part of 1930 and neither its astronomical nor its astrological character has as yet been fully determined.

It is considered by some that its name indicates a connection with Scorpio, and it may even be claimed as ruler of that sign.

Preliminary observations, based on such data as are available, lead the present writer to consider that its action is such as to cause hidden and subterranean states to break forth or erupt, like earthquakes or volcanoes, bringing about a climax in the life with much disturbance and upheaval, followed by calmer and more wholesome conditions. This may occur in mundane affairs and circumstances, or it may operate in the emotions; but in either case it will be analogous to the above-mentioned geological phenomena. Thus it is often the planet of the "healing crisis".

It seems by its action to indicate the opening and ending of chapters in the life as well as of life itself.

It indicates isolation.

§ 12. BASIC PSYCHOLOGICAL CONCEPTS

The understanding of the planets will be easier after the student has obtained a clear idea of the meanings of the elements, as explained in the next chapter. We may, however, now tabulate some of the chief concepts connected with them:

	GOOD	BAD
The Sun . . .	"Personality" Leadership Magnanimity	"Side", bluff, bombast Favouritism

	GOOD	BAD
The Moon . .	Sympathy	Timidity
	Protectiveness	Clannishness and prejudice
	Prudence	Sentimentality
	Love of home and country	
Mercury . . .	Intellect	Dishonesty, lying, bad temper
	Powers of expression	
Venus . . .	Content	Apathy
	Harmony	Indolence, peace at any price
	Affection	Lack of moral stamina
Mars . . .	Courage	Quarrelsomeness, roughness
	Energy	Destructiveness
		Egotism
Jupiter . . .	Hope	Over-optimism
	Generosity	Waste
	High spirits	Horse-play
	Piety	Empty verbiage
Saturn . . .	Prudence	Lack of vision
	Self-control	Narrowness
	Practicality	Worldliness
		Self-centredness
Uranus . . .	Originality	Perversity
	Genius	Eccentricity
	Force of character	Self-will
Neptune . . .	Inspiration	Utopianism
	Spirituality	Worry
		Deception
Pluto . . .	Aloofness	Loneliness
	Publicity	Ruthlessness

The expression of the higher side of each planet is easy or difficult according to the general tenor of the nativity and the particular strength of the planet itself, especially (so far as character goes) with regard to the sign it occupies.

At the same time the student will not need to be told that no sensible person will seriously try to make planetary configurations a justification for moral failings. Bad positions do, to a certain extent, provide an excuse for our faults and render them understandable when they would not otherwise be, but, while they may make the attainment of a high moral standard difficult, they can never make it impossible; and the astrologer, being one to whom much is given, is also one from whom much may legitimately be required. Many fine characters have much-afflicted maps.

Further, note that although the "influences" of the planets have been given above in terms of mind and character, it does not follow that they always work in that manner, as we shall see later. They are, however, *essentially* the same, upon whatever plane they operate.

CHAPTER FOUR

THE QUALITIES, ELEMENTS AND SIGNS IN DETAIL

§ 1. THEIR MUTUAL RELATIONS

WE have enumerated the classes into which the signs are divided in Chapter One. A more careful study of these divisions is now requisite, for we may safely say that, from the psychological standpoint, if not from that of fate or destiny, the qualities and elements are of primary importance. Indeed, although they are but seven in number, the student who has got a clear conception of what they stand for will have gone a very long way towards understanding the astrology of character.

Reference should be made to the table on page 18.

Note that the four mutable signs are ruled by Mercury and Jupiter, which rule these and no others, so that they may be considered purely mutable in nature. On the other hand the Sun-Moon (which two bodies must for the purpose of psychological study be treated as the positive and negative aspects of one principle, as indeed they are), Venus, Mars, and Saturn each rule one cardinal and one fixed sign. Hence there is no such thing as exclusively cardinal or fixed planetary force.

Then, again, we have seen in the last chapter that the fire-water signs, on the one hand, and air-earth on the other, are grouped apart by the fact that no planet rules one of each class.

To illustrate these points we may reproduce the table on page 18, but substituting the planetary rulers for the signs:

			FIRE	WATER	AIR	EARTH
Cardinal	.	.	Mars	Moon	Venus	Saturn
Fixed	.	.	Sun	Mars	Saturn	Venus
Mutable	.	.	Jupiter		Mercury	

§ 2. THE QUALITIES

These are also called the Quadruplicities, because each comprises four signs. This, in fact, is their true astrological name; the use of the term Qualities is derived from the Gunas or Qualities of Hindu philosophy and has been introduced by astrologers of the theosophic school. They are also sometimes referred to as the Three Modes.

The *Cardinal Signs* stand for Activity, or Doing. They show free manifestation in the outer world, and produce energy, push, and enterprise.

Under affliction the cardinal signs show the restless and inconstant busybody, always beginning new projects and then forsaking them, without any settled policy, and given to interfering freely with others. Absence of this quality causes lack of initiative and lethargy.

The *Fixed Signs* are concerned chiefly with Feeling and the "pleasure-pain" aspect of things. Thus where a cardinal person would ask with regard to something fresh, "How will it affect what I want to do?" the fixed person would ask: "Is it pleasant or disagreeable?"

The fixed sign persons are conservative, stable, set in their habits and opinions, strong in their likes and dislikes, and obstinate. They change seldom, but when they do their changes are often drastic.

Under affliction they are lazy, self-indulgent, stubborn, bigoted, and stupid.

Lack of the quality shows absence of principle, ballast, and consistency.

The *Mutable Signs* are intermediate between the two other qualities, having something of each. They stand for Thought and the impartial mental attitude towards things, seeking to understand without bias. They are usually clever, mentally quick and alert, adaptable, changeful, and what is still called "mercurial". They represent those who study and write about the actions of others, rather than themselves trying to "make history". The expression "common signs" is sometimes used by reason of their having something in common with the other two qualities.

We may mention in illustration some of the social types that come under these qualities.

Cardinal.—Leaders and men of action, pioneers, people with a goal and purpose in life.

Fixed.—The landowners and squires, and to a large extent the proprietors of old-established conservative businesses, as apart from the Cardinal people who build them up. Most officials and people who "occupy positions", especially those involving the exercise of authority and upholding of rules and regulations rather than finding out new ways and means.

Mutable.—All go-betweens, agents, and commissionmen; students of all sorts; inventors, writers, publishers, journalists; those who describe and comment upon the doings of others, but are themselves impersonal; philosophers and men of science, literature, and art.

It is to be observed that a quality or element is predominant or deficient according to the number of planets in signs of that nature, and as well as the planets we must include the Ascendant. Planets themselves can also, by their prominence, make up for lack of an element or quality. Thus a person with Mercury rising would never lack the mutable quality, and one with the Sun rising would always possess a certain amount of fire, whatever else the map might contain. This point is important.

The qualities are not difficult to understand, despite their profound significance.

We now pass on to the elements or triplicities.

§ 3. The Elements

The *Fiery Element* comprises Aries, Leo, and Sagittarius. Its function is self-assertion and active manifestation. It is positive, forceful, self-confident, and aggressive; inclined to faith and optimism; fond of good living, sport, exercise, company, and adventure; always ready for what is new, and never afraid to face hazards and take the chances of life and circumstances.

The faults are such as spring from too robust, vigorous, and exuberant life, such as extravagance and all sorts of excess, recklessness, overhopefulness, pride, arrogance, coarse animal spirits, and lack of sympathy for the weak.

Without fire the native tends to lack enthusiasm, spirits, *joie de vivre*, and vitality; he becomes matter-of-fact, humdrum, and over-serious.

The *Water Signs* are Cancer, Scorpio, and Pisces. They are the opposite of fire, and show the shrinking, fearful, self-protective instinct, without which fire would cause life, whether in man or beast, to exhaust itself with sheer extravagance of vigour, or destroy itself through lack of prudence and excess of confidence.

The virtues of water are therefore prudence and foresight, sympathy and the desire to shield and protect, whilst its failings are such as arise from timidity, suspicion, fearfulness, or distrust of self and others. Scorpio, being ruled by Mars, shows the timidity least; nevertheless, though physically courageous if put to the test, it inclines to suspiciousness and self-repression. All the water signs are sensitive and tend to keep themselves and their feelings to themselves, while fire is always self-expressive.

It will be seen that a horoscopic clash between fire and water denotes much inharmony, the two elements rending the native's nature asunder in the attempt to express on the one hand and repress on the other.

Fire and water are largely primitive and instinctive, having to do with our spontaneous emotions and impulses rather than with deliberately planned ideas. Earth and air are mental and purposive, the one being the executant, the other the designer.

Air is intellectual, refined, thoughtful, and devoted to the arts and sciences, especially from the more abstract and theoretical point of view. Its virtues lie in its idealism and desire for truth. It is co-operative, unitive, and harmonious in action, and is perhaps best seen in the domain of pure intellect. By itself it tends to become divorced from the real and practical, and to spend its time in day-dreaming; it works with ideas rather than concrete objects, and, in the case of the less evolved, merely gives some artistic taste without either energy or ability to make use of it. When the practical part of the horoscope is also well developed there is considerable power for both planning and carrying out great works, and we get the practical engineer, designer, architect, and social and religious idealist.

Earth represents the brain applied to material ends, and is the craftsman, builder, and practical scientist. It may be said that civilization, in its material aspects, is chiefly the work of this element, which has raised us from the animal to the mastery of the physical world. The same lack of idealism and respect for the abstract and spiritual sides of life that we note in modern civilization is the fault of earth, when unredeemed by air. It becomes materialistic, sordid, commonplace, utilitarian in a narrow sense, and a slave to routine, law and order. It is a limiting element, and those who are largely composed, astrologically, of earth tend to be dry, matter-of-fact, and circumscribed in their outlook. On the other hand, lack of earth produces inability to bring forth tangible and useful results.

We pass now to a consideration of the signs.

§ 4. THE SIGNS IN DETAIL

We have seen on page 18 that the twelve signs are, from one point of view, the outcome of dividing the zodiac into four elements and each element into three signs, one of each quality.

Observe that fire and water, being emotional, have much in common with the fixed quality, while air and earth, being mental have much in common with the mutable. Hence a sign that belongs to an element congenial to its quality produces a very marked action of that nature. As, for example, Gemini, which is mutable-air, and therefore very intellectual in its manifestation, while Pisces, mutable-water, has no such similarity of element and quality, and produces consequently an unsettled temperament, the mind and feeling both being active and sometimes at variance.

DOUBLE SIGNS

Gemini, Sagittarius, and Pisces are traditionally called "double". They are characterized by restlessness and lack of concentration and one-pointedness. Both in life and character they show a curious doubleness. Thus there are often two separate vocations, either at the same time or consecutively, and frequently two marriages. These signs also tend to produce twins.

We shall now set forth in twelve short essays the leading characteristics of the signs. It is necessary to learn to blend these values with those of the planets that may occupy the signs, and, in the case of the signs being on the ascendant, to take into consideration the position of the ruler of that sign by house and sign, and its aspects. It will be seen that no textbook can deal with all possible combinations, but, by studying the principles involved, the student will be able to judge these as he meets them.

These essays are mainly written of the signs when on the ascendant, *but a stronger and truer effect is usually seen when the Sun occupies a sign*, whilst the Moon's sign-position manifests through the instinctive and impulsive nature, and is also to a large extent the vehicle for the transmission of inherited traits and also those habits which are acquired in childhood from family-associations.

The Sun shows the man as a self-conscious individual; the Moon is the "natural man"; the ascending sign is the nexus between character and body.

ARIES ♈

This is a cardinal-fire sign, the positive sign of Mars and the exaltation of the Sun. It represents the crude outrush of manifesting life, and is characterized by extreme activity, especially physical. There is unlimited energy, daring, love of enterprise and adventure, and a quick, decided temper that ill brooks any opposition or restraint. In good types the courage and vigour are devoted to sensible and useful ends, and the native may achieve much as a reformer or advocate of the weak. In bad types the native is quarrelsome, "spoils for a fight", will not compromise, and sees only his own point of view. The daring becomes foolhardiness, and there is an entire lack of common prudence and foresight. There are disastrous outbreaks of temper and feats of empty bravado, and the native is liable to be victimized by anyone who cares to arouse him by taunts or provocative challenges. Aries rarely looks before it leaps, and there are few natives of the sign who do not, at some time or another, do foolish and short-sighted things. The mind is often quick and able in dealing with concrete things, but it is essentially a sign of action, ignores theoretical considerations, and it likes to rely on the inspiration of the moment to see things through. It is a good advocate, but a poor judge, for it finds impartiality difficult.

TAURUS ♉

The negative sign of Venus and exaltation of the Moon. Fixed-earth.

This is in most respects the opposite of Aries. It is slow, careful, steady, practical, and reserved. It tends to inertia, and is often lazy, sensuous, and selfish. It is easily contented, and enjoys the simple things of life, especially those of a rural nature. It is motherly, homely, and protective. In business it is conservative, and likes safe and well-tried methods. In good types there is much patience, perseverance, firmness, and determination, but these are often negative and passive virtues, and the native will do little without definite stimulus. It makes a good administrator, and can keep order and discipline easily. There is usually a high sense of probity, especially in all matters concerning money. The temper is peaceable and not easily roused, but when once provoked Taurus can be violent and unrelenting.

There is a good sense of colour and of tune, and the sign produces many fine singers. Otherwise it tends to agricultural pursuits, and seems commoner and truer to type in the country than in towns.

It is well to add that the above description is based in the main on traditional accounts of the sign; but that the present writer has found many natives of Taurus to conform much more nearly to the purely Venus type, being gentle, affectionate, sensitive, and cultured.

GEMINI ♊

Gemini is an airy or intellectual sign, and is ruled by Mercury.

It is pre-eminently the sign connected with the concrete mind, or that part of the mind which deals with facts and figures rather than with ideals and experiments. It is the sign of reason and logic, and Geminians excel all others in their ability to grasp conceptions clearly and logically. Hazy or sentimental thinking, leading to loose or inaccurate conclusions, are particularly distasteful to them, and, while able to deal with abstractions, and usually interested in literature and art, they are always capable of examining things from the rational standpoint without any emotional bias. They are more matter-of-fact than sentimental, and admire and like brain and cleverness. They are nearly always mentally active themselves and are quick at repartee, being bright and energetic conversationalists, good debaters, and keen at argument. There is much mental vivacity and agility.

The faults of the sign are lack of concentration and the tendency to take on too many projects and enterprises, so that they have "too many irons in the fire", and leave things unfinished. Only when this diffuse tendency is overcome can the sign get the most from its fine intellectual powers. There is lack of decision and a good deal of wavering and a difficulty in making up the mind. The Geminian often excels in detail, and may lose himself in it, failing to "see the wood on account of the trees". Emotionally there is a distinct tendency to egoism, hardness, and selfishness, Gemini people being too mental to develop warmth of heart. Even when the rest of the nativity shows generosity of feeling, it cannot manifest freely and easily through Gemini. There is often too great a liking for introspection, with resultant self-centredness and discontent. There is sometimes flippancy and irreverence.

Under severe afflictions there may be deceit, untruthfulness, or dishonesty.

Physically Gemini is very active, the limbs, eyes, and expression being in constant change. They are restless and changeful, seldom settling down. In many respects they resemble children and retain their youth for long. They often dislike old people, but at the same time, are not fond of young children, and make bad mothers or nurses, owing to their highly strung nervous system.

They come much into contact with books and writings, and make excellent clerks, teachers, and students. Their happiest days are often those spent at school and college, where they easily hold their own.

CANCER ♋

This is a cardinal-water sign, ruled by the Moon.

Cancerians are noted for their extreme sensitiveness, both physical and emotional. They are commonly moody, and at the same time, owing to their cardinal quality, their moods vary rapidly, usually reflecting each outside influence with which they come into contact. This is particularly true of Cancer *rising*; the Sun in Cancer has a steadying effect. The primitive type is emotional, and sentimental, while its sensitiveness renders it extremely timid and even helpless. There may be morbidity and sensationalism. The advanced type shows the same sensitiveness, but has control of its feelings, and, while retaining deep and ready sympathies, is more judicious and discriminating in expressing them.

The imagination is vivid and Cancer natives enter easily into other people's feelings and thoughts, and sense "atmospheres" readily. There is humour, of the "pawky" sort, dry and kindly.

In primitive types of all the water signs there is danger of moral weakness, owing to the activity of the sensational nature and the ease with which impressions of all sorts are absorbed. Cancer is, however, to a certain extent paradoxical. It is the sign of the "Eternal feminine", and, just as women are in one aspect weak, and in the other courageous and able to endure pain and suffering that the more positive male could not undergo, so Cancerians may show much tenacity and passive bravery, especially when the maternal or protective side of the nature is roused. They have the greatest sticking power of the signs, and once they have taken up a position or idea they maintain it with a persistence which is not found in more objective signs.

They are usually good business people, being shrewd, thrifty, prudent, and careful. They proceed cautiously and often almost imperceptibly, without much noise or self-advertisement, except in so far as business may require.

The domestic side is usually strong; they are home-loving and devoted to their families. Often there is much clannishness, prejudice against strangers, and a tendency to make the family the end of their existences. The love of the past and of old things is strong; the memory is retentive, and thoughts hark back readily to the past, in which they often live, while regarding the future with anxiety and misgiving.

Leo ♌

The sign Leo is of the fixed quality, and belongs to the fire element, being ruled by the Sun.

It is probably the sign of the Zodiac which possesses the greatest amount of *power*, using that word in the widest sense. Physically there is usually great vitality, and the same characteristic applies equally to the mental and emotional natures. There is usually some degree of ambition and a firm will, with considerable persistence, and, since these are usually united to a naturally effective personality, we seldom find the native of Leo occupying an obscure position. The inherent ability of the sign brings it forward and upward until it has achieved a position of prominence and authority, even though the native may not have any special talent. If, however, the nativity also shows real mental acuteness and judgment the native will go far. Few "born leaders" are without a strong solar influence, either through the Sun itself, or its sign, or both. Leo never likes to work in corners; its destiny is to come to the front, deal with large issues, and leave drudgery and detail to others. It possesses all the gifts of the born commander, and produces people whom others readily respect and obey. Usually genial and often democratic in theory, its methods are nearly always autocratic. The tendency to delegate work is very strong in nearly all Leos, but in good types the Leo himself always remains, not a mere figure-head, but a real director and inspirer. Naturally in weak types this characteristic is easily perverted, and we get the kind of person who tries to win praise for himself from what has been done by humbler members of the zodiacal fellowship working under him.

The Leonian is temperamentally good-natured, obliging, and often even devotedly affectionate, but an element of patronage often creeps into his attitude towards others. While making a good and open-handed master, there is often little inclination to regard others as equals, so that independent natures find the sign irritating in its attitude towards them. On the other hand, weak and clinging natures find it a tower of help and strength, ever ready to pour out life, courage, and confidence from its own abundant stores.

The faults of the sign are those common to weak natures highly placed. They develop vanity, are easily flattered, surround themselves with favourites, aim at show rather than merit, and become assuming, snobbish, and worldly, promising much and achieving little. There may be secret meanness beneath an appearance of pompous self-satisfaction.

VIRGO ♍

This is the negative sign of Mercury, and is mutable-earth.

Its keynote may be said to be practical mentality, or the brain applied to concrete matters. Although usually artistic and literary, and gifted with considerable taste, Virginians seldom lack appreciation of the facts of life; they are generally careful in money-matters, and possess sound commercial instinct. They are neat, methodical, precise, and without regard for show or pretenticusness, preferring to judge and be judged by results. They take a pride in their work, if it is at all congenial to them, and as a rule like to be left alone to carry out their tasks in peace and quiet. The abilities are great for all work requiring good mental powers, conscientiousness, and attention to detail; they make excellent secretaries, or subordinates of any kind, but do not often assume control, dislike responsibility on a large scale, and shrink from the limelight and self-advertisement; in fact, they are often shy and retiring, making few friends, being particular about whom they meet socially.

They usually possess skill in manual craftsmanship, and either for a livelihood or a hobby cultivate such things as carving, metal-work, clock-making, or engineering. They are also often literary and possess unusual humour and whimsicality. Gardening also generally attracts them, and another characteristic is the marked interest in matters pertaining to health, diet, and hygiene. They may be doctors or physical culturists, and at times degenerate into valetudinarians.

Virgo is pre-eminently a sign of criticism and discrimination, especially as regards details, and the commonest failings of the sign are the outcome of this tendency. They may be chronic fault-finders, cantankerous, prejudiced, and narrow in their views, with the result that they are unpopular with those who misunderstand their natures. The love of method also leads to fussiness and immersion in detail, and their refinement may develop into prudery and lack of charity towards the lapses of warmer-blooded signs. At the same time many natives of Virgo are notably kind and ready to oblige those whom they recognize as friends.

LIBRA ♎

This is the positive sign of Venus and the exaltation of Saturn, and is cardinal air.

The outstanding characteristics are love of harmony, justice, and sympathy for pain and suffering. There is a highly developed sense of beauty. Librans are very sociable and companionable; they seldom lead separative lives, and are always found doing their best work and achieving most happiness when associated with others, either in marriage or in some other form of partnership, such as a close friendship. They are affable, courteous, obliging, and very rarely guilty of a desire to injure others.

At the same time they are not fond of rough, ugly, or dirty conditions, and do not care to expose themselves to the more sordid aspects of life, so that they are ill-fitted for work that involves unpleasant associations.

The temper is even and equable, and if ruffled subsides readily. They never bear malice; in fact, the memory is inclined to be short, and there is a readiness on all occasions to forgive and forget. They find a disturbed or quarrelsome atmosphere hard to support, and give way or compromise rather than face prolonged discord. Hence they may seem shallow and insincere.

In evolved types there is much sweetness and spirituality; it is said that Libra alone of the signs can "touch pitch and not be defiled"; even the most primitive types can generally respond to better things when an opportunity is given, and in many cases there is a marked longing for escape from worldly conditions, and a good deal of secret unhappiness in the face of the roughness and hardship of life.

They are rarely extreme in their views and are impartial; and on this account they are valuable as go-betweens, emissaries of peace, and agents of all sorts, always working for harmony and the establishment of harmonious relationships.

The liking for the opposite sex is usually noticeable.

The faults are those of weakness and compliancy. They find it hard to say "No", or to take a firm attitude in the face of hostility, and tend to avoid unpleasantness at all costs. Hence they compromise too much, "sit on the fence", and waver from one view to another without giving a downright reply which would commit them to one course. They are often lazy, and, while high types dress tastefully and well, the primitive ones may be slovenly and careless. They cannot act on their own responsibility, but instinctively seek a partner.

It is to be noted that the *Sun in Libra* differs widely from Libra rising and is more energetic. It is also a position of disputatiousness and even of warfare, being common in the horoscopes of generals, public debaters, and propagandists; it is as loth to give way as Libra rising is prone to do so.

SCORPIO ♏

The negative sign of Mars, and that of fixed water.

There is an intense emotional nature. No sign has more profound and enduring feelings, for owing to the fixity of Scorpio these become set, with the result that in high types there is unwavering devotion to principles, deep sympathy, and true understanding, while in primitives, in whom the moral standard is low or uncertain, a host of dangerous feelings may appear— bitter dislikes or hatreds, often cherished for a lifetime, extreme sensitiveness to imagined slights or injustice, resentment, suspicion, and furious anger. Scorpios of this kind are very prone to think themselves under-valued, and to relieve their feelings on this score in the shape of constant boasting. There may be treachery, cruelty, and revengefulness. Sometimes these worse traits appear in childhood, but die out with good training. There are nearly always strong affections, and great care should be taken in training a Scorpio child that these are not ruined either by over-indulgence on the one hand, or harshness on the other. The physical endurance is great, but the emotional nature needs careful treatment.

The sign is extremely thorough-going, and few flabby characters are born under it. There is usually courage, and also energy and capacity for toil in the pursuit of any aim which claims the native's devotion. As a result many heroes have been born under the sign, as well as many notable villains. They do nothing by halves, and, having once selected their course in life, pursue it relentlessly.

In primitives there may be reckless self-indulgence and in evolved ones intense devotion. The powerful feelings constantly tempt the native, and few Scorpios pass through life without having run the full gamut of temptation on the physical plane. Self-control and self-denial are the chief virtues that they need to develop.

The better types are noticeably dignified and endowed with self-respect and proper pride; they are often grave and restrained in their speech and demeanour, and do not readily unbend.

It is a sign that frequently gives an inclination towards some form of mysticism or occultism, and it is prominent in most enthusiastic Freemasons. There is a natural tendency towards what is secret and hidden, and a love of probing mysteries and getting at the bottom of things.

They excel as detectives, inspectors, and investigators of all kinds, make good surgeons and chemists, and frequently enter the Army or Navy.

SAGITTARIUS ♐

This is a mutable-fire sign, and is ruled by Jupiter.

Typical Sagittarians are high-spirited, kind, generous, and honest, with a great love of outdoor life, sports, and athletics. They enjoy life to the full, and are always ready for convivial amusements of all sorts. The mental abilities are also as a rule above the average, and in good types there may be interest in philosophy, metaphysics, and religion, this being particularly true of the Sun in the sign. There is a love of travelling, exploring, and wandering, and the sense of home is usually small.

Freedom and personal liberty make a strong appeal, but at the same time most Sagittarians also understand the need of law and order, and have no inclination towards violence.

The faults of the sign are the result of its exuberance of life and spirits, and its restlessness and love of covering large stretches of country, both physically and mentally. There may be extravagance, carelessness over detail, waste, exaggeration, too great faith in luck, superficiality, a tendency to know a little of everything but all of nothing, with sudden crazes for people, intellectual interests, and hobbies, which blaze up and die away, and also a certain degree of loudness and vulgarity.

It is, however, on the whole, one of the most fortunate and likeable of the signs, and even primitive examples are seldom anyone's enemy but their own.

CAPRICORN ♑

This is the negative sign of Saturn and the exaltation of Mars.

The *Sun in Capricorn* tends to produce a good Saturn type, careful, prudent, conscientious, ambitious, but just to others, justice being sometimes more pronounced than mercy.

The failings which may occur in weak examples are such as worldliness, snobbishness, a tendency to manage and even to make use of others for private ends, narrowness of outlook, too great respect for the past and a refusal to change with the times and to progress. There may be downright selfishness and craftiness in pursuit of personal advantage. The general abilities are usually good but are commonly limited to so-called practical things.

Capricorn rising seems to give a much more emotional and introspective type, a love of music or other forms of art being a common characteristic. The conscientiousness and practical abilities are less, so that this position will often produce clever but ineffective people, who seem unable to find their right place in the world and in consequence fret and flit capriciously from one thing to another, achieving little and often becoming hard to please, sour and disappointed. It is a restless and sometimes rather self-important position and many examples are loquacious and pushing, disliking to be overlooked.

The earlier part of the sign when rising often indicates a kind, humane nature, sometimes markedly religious.

Sun in Capricorn is often successful in scientific work, whereas Capricorn rising tends rather to the arts.

AQUARIUS ♒

This is the positive sign of Saturn, by some held to be ruled by Uranus. It is fixed-air.

The purely Saturnian Aquarian resembles the Capricornian in his seriousness and his grave outlook on life, but he is as a rule less practical; the mind is more idealistic and may spend much time in abstract thoughts and theoretical speculations, often on problems of philosophy, religion, and sociology, and the result may be a lack of practical common sense. On the other hand, there is nearly always kindness, sympathy, and refinement, together with an intense love for and feeling of kinship with wild nature. There is generally artistic ability. The native tends to be attracted to societies, clubs, associations, groups of people, and "movements" of all sorts, easily merging his own personality in "causes". There are many associates, but the temperament is often too detached to make warm friendships.

Aquarius has a great love of personal freedom and resents enforced obedience, but apart from this it is usually faithful, constant, and affectionate. But, above all, it is the sign of truth and sincerity, and will not act a conventional lie, and it is this trait which sometimes leads it in direct opposition to ordinary ideas of morality and may get it a reputation for looseness among those who are attached to the form rather than the reality. Uranus resembles Aquarius in this lack of conventional bias, but it is more uncontrolled in its hatred of restraint, having a Martian resentment and energy that seem foreign to the usually friendly and sympathetic Aquarian. At the same time Aquarians, when their nativities show violent afflictions, especially by Mars to Saturn or Uranus, may espouse extreme opinions, and such types are often accused of inconsistency and lack of straightforwardness.

It is pre-eminently the *human* sign, and the very fact that it signifies mankind in general makes it hard to specify particular characteristics.

It should be recollected that in these latitudes nearly all persons with Aquarian ascendants have Pisces intercepted in the 1st house, and if there is a planet in that sign and none in Aquarius, both appearance and character will be to some extent Piscean.

PISCES ♓

The negative sign of Jupiter, with strong affinity to Neptune, and the exaltation of Venus.

Pisces is the most negative and plastic of the signs, and it seldom possesses a very strong individual character, for it lives largely on the thoughts and feelings of those with whom it comes into contact. Hence it is, above all, the actor's sign, giving great ability to absorb and express the emotions of others. The imagination is extremely active, as in all watery signs, and the life is often passed in the imaginative rather than the actual world. Hence the sign is frequently prominent in the nativities of writers, poets, and artists.

The religious nature is often highly developed. The sympathies are abundant, and the sign is attracted to the needy and sick and all those who require help. It may cause the native to connect himself with hospitals, asylums, or other refuges and institutions of a like description, as well as prisons, monasteries, and other places of a solitary nature.

In some types the desire to help others seems to find expression in the giving of advice and the preaching of "sermons" in and out of season.

There is usually much affection for animals and love of the sea.

Pisceans are commonly jovial and convivial and make entertaining companions. They vary from the highest to the lowest spirits, and are equally ready to help others and themselves to apply for assistance, being often without much sense of responsibility, thriftless, unmethodical, and devoid of worldly wisdom. Indeed, a large proportion of life's wastrels are born under this sign, while it has undoubtedly produced some of the most spiritual characters of history. They are as a rule their own worst enemies, and, though not violent or cruel, Pisces is capable of deceiving both itself and others, and produces bad examples of hypocrisy, especially of the religious kind.

Drugs have a great fascination for many Pisceans, who seem to crave emotional and physical stimulation, but their physique is frequently by no means strong and indulgence in this direction generally produces rapid collapse. It is therefore, above all, necessary that they should carefully avoid the formation of habits of this character.

Sometimes the affinity between Pisces and drugs appears as an interest in chemistry, especially from the medicinal point of view.

CHAPTER FIVE

THE HOUSES IN DETAIL

§ I

THE Houses are divisions of the visible heavens, as seen at any point of time at any place on the earth, with a corresponding division of the invisible heavens, hidden beneath the earth.

Every department of human life falls under one or other of the Twelve Houses. They are channels, so to speak, through which man enters into relationship with his environment. They have more distinct reference to physical things than the planets and signs, which are connected rather with the character and disposition. Yet mind, emotions, body, and circumstances act and re-act continuously and we cannot say definitely that any factor of the horoscope is *exclusively* related to one of these only.

Thus it is commonly said that the Sun, Moon, and planets may be taken to correspond to Spirit, the Signs to the Soul, and the Houses to the Body. But, whilst this may be true in an analogical sense, it will not be found very helpful in practical astrology. Some house-positions, for example, affect the character very markedly, as, for instance, a rising planet or a planet in the 3rd, and bodies in signs often have a quite material effect.

The correspondence between the Houses and the Signs is very easily traced.

We must affirm our opinion that, in the study of nativities, the equal method of division[1] yields better results than any other. It is asserted, indeed, that if any other system is used,

---

[1] See concluding section of chapter.

deductions from house-position will often be misleading and inaccurate. Nevertheless, this is a matter of dissension amongst astrologers and each student must form his own opinion.

THE FIRST HOUSE

This rules the physical body, considered as the instrument through which the higher principles that make up man manifest materially. It affects health, temperament, and the physical build and appearance.

Everything that is in the horoscope has to manifest in everyday life *via* the rising sign, or sign on the cusp of the 1st house, which thus becomes a kind of lens through which all influences have to pass, suffering modification in doing so. Thus the 1st affects the more obvious and easily noticed part of the disposition; it shows the person as he or she appears to the casual acquaintance, and denotes the *manners* of the individual, as much as any one part of the nativity may be said to do so.

THE SECOND HOUSE

This rules possessions of all kinds; the material that goes to the support of the living body shown by the 1st, the financial condition and the native's attitude towards money, and his worldly resources.

It has some influence on his *feelings*, and what may be called true character, or principle, and must be taken into consideration in judging these things, especially if planets are in it.

THE THIRD HOUSE

This concerns relations and relationships and all means of intercommunication (upon which, of course, relationships depend, since one cannot be related to a thing without a means of maintaining communication with it). Thus we have blood-relations, especially brothers and sisters;[1] letters, books, and writing of all sorts; short journeys (those that are of a routine rather than an explorative kind); all things that are used for such journeys, as trams, bicycles, and motors; and, above all, speech, with which we are able to bring our own mind into contact with those of others.

Education also comes under this house, and the Mind generally is much influenced by it, as we shall see in Chapter Six.

THE FOURTH HOUSE

Like all three watery houses (i.e., 4th, 8th, and 12th, which correspond to the watery signs), this has a deep and abstruse signification. It denotes both the beginning and the end of life, the womb and the grave; it stands for all that is indrawn and secluded, and thus acquires as one of its commonest meanings that of the Home or the Private Life, and so it governs houses, land, and the early life at home. It is connected with the parents, and, paradoxically, is said to denote the father, although it corresponds to Cancer, ruled by the Moon.

It is questionable whether any house shows the parents of the native very clearly, but since both the vocation, public life, and status on the one hand, and the home-life on the other, depend largely on them, the meridian line (which is the cusps of the 4th and 10th) reflects to a considerable extent the dispositions and fortunes of the parents. Other factors affecting the parents will be explained in Chapter Seven, § 5.

THE FIFTH HOUSE

Joys, pleasures, holidays, courtship, and all sorts of enterprises and new undertakings come under this house, as well

---

[1] Traditionally. But the author has never found the 3rd house to be a reliable index to the brothers and sisters of the native. It is safer to take the 4th as a general pointer to family conditions.

as speculation and games of hazard; also the birth of children and the native's own children and grandchildren[1]. It is the house that corresponds to Leo, and through it the great creative and joy-engendering activities of the Sun find expression.

It denotes all objects of the native's *instinctive* affections, and thus is often indicative of the playmates, pets, and sweethearts. Seriously afflicted, it may denote immorality, self-indulgence, profligacy, and all kinds of looseness due to desire for pleasure.

Nevertheless it is traditionally regarded as a fortunate house, being in trine to the first.

The Sixth House

In contradistinction to the 5th this is said to be the house of work and toil of all sorts, by which the pleasures of the 5th are fed, just as the 2nd house feeds the Arietic forces of the 1st. It governs subordinates, servants of all kinds, and service. Hence, in so far as we subordinate ourselves to anything, whether it is an ideal or a person, we identify our activities with this house.

It is called the house of health, but the bodily well-being cannot, as will be explained, be judged solely from it.

It must be regarded as an unfortunate house wherein good planets are weak and evil ones incline to moodiness, pessimism, and sometimes to ill-temper, for it has a relation with the moods.

The Seventh House

Under this comes the principle of *partnership* in all its manifestations. Generally its influence is good, and it shows the husband or wife, the business partner, if any, and bosom-friends.

---

[1] In that branch of Astrology known as Horary the grandchildren are placed under the 9th house, as being the fifth from the 5th. But in natal astrology the 5th has a general value in regard to one's descendants, much more marked in some cases than in others.

Under affliction it may, however, assume a hostile significance, and show open enemies. It is the *other party* to all our bargains and in all negotiations.

It would be a grave error to regard it, as is commonly the case, as affecting only one's married life; it determines to a very large extent how we "get on" with people in general.

It shows our ideal self, what we *would* be in contradistinction to the 1st house, which shows what we *are*, and it signifies what is complementary to and lacking in ourselves, and therefore is required by us in a partner to render us complete, and is dangerous to us in an enemy, because we lack it ourselves.

THE EIGHTH HOUSE

Traditionally the house of death. It shows the interplay of decay and regeneration, both physical and moral, the death of the old and the birth of new things from the ruins. It has significance in relation to health and accidents, and probably rules the effects that others have on one's health, as by infection and suggestion.

Planets in this house affect the corporature, according to their natures, and this is frequently very marked if the planet is close to the cusp. Thus Jupiter inclines to obesity and Saturn to spareness and often to shortness of stature.

In the nativities of immoral and criminal types, this house, if heavily afflicted planets are in it, may show crime and retribution; in the maps of ordinary worldly people it shows the property of the partner and money owed to the native, or his money in the hands of others.

It rules the goods of the dead, legacies, wills and settlements, and all occupations that have to do with death, such as undertaking and the meat trade.

Although this does not appear to have been noticed by other writers, planets in this sector strongly affect character, acting much as do bodies in the 6th house. That is to say, through the moods and impulses.

It is related to the sexual nature.

THE NINTH HOUSE

This rules travel and exploration—long journeys into unknown places; also *mental* exploration, as in metaphysical and philosophic thinking and speculative thought of all sorts. It rules foreign countries, the churches, and the law, as well as persons and things related to them.

It has much to do with inspiration and man's relation with spiritual things and beings. It is said to be connected with prophecy and with dreams.

It has bearing on man's moral ideals and conscience.

THE TENTH HOUSE

This is the house wherein the physical and mundane activities of the native reach their pinnacle. It indicates the native's place in society, his standing before the world, and so, in part, his sense of honour, his ambitions, and his vocation, which last is frequently the result of his ambition and is the determinant, to a great extent, of his social status.

It is said to denote the Mother, but this is often questioned; see in this connection what is said above under the 4th house.

It shows those in authority over the native.

THE ELEVENTH HOUSE

This rules the hopes and aspirations, the joys of the spiritual and intellectual part of the native, as the 5th stands for his pleasures on the lower side.

It shows the friends of the native and his associations with others in clubs, societies, and so forth.

It denotes his *spiritual and intellectual* aspirations; in other words, his ideals.

It is deemed a fortunate house.

THE TWELFTH HOUSE

Traditionally this signifies sorrows, confinement, secret enemies, betrayals, and ambushes. Its sorrows are mainly caused by others, or affect others directly and the native indirectly because of his associations with the sufferers. In material things it is a house of disappointment, limitation and loss, unless strongly tenanted, but in a spiritual sense it is indicative of self-sacrifice and the forsaking of worldly things for the life of the spirit.

Strong planets in this house usually give eventual success, as they are carried towards the meridian by direction (see Chapter Ten), but the beginnings of life are often humble.

As the sixth house from the Seventh, the Twelfth is specially concerned with the health of the partner. It may also denote the native's illnesses, in so far as they cause confinement (especially in homes, hospitals, and similar institutions). The illnesses of this house are usually longer than those of the Sixth.

I have found the 12th, as being the end of one life-circle and the starting-point of the next, to be very frequently a good index to the asc. of the eldest child. So far as I know, this observation has not been made previously.

It is worthy of observation that the last six houses tend to operate on a wider and more general scale than the first six. Thus, 1st house=the personal self, 7th=the public; the 2nd=one's own property, the 8th=money of others associated with the native; 3rd=short journeys of a routine character, 9th=long and explorative journeys; 4th=home, 10th=vocation and standing; 5th=pleasures (always limited), 11th=ideals (infinite); 6th=personal health, 12th=sorrows through others. The last six nearly always *involve other people*.

Houses are in all cases judged:

(*a*) By their *essential rulers*, or those bodies which rule the corresponding sign.

(*b*) By their *accidental rulers*, or those bodies ruling the sign on the cusp or intercepted.

(*c*) By their *occupants*, or the planets placed in them, if any.

(*d*) By aspects to the cusp.

The essential rulers commonly denote the native's attitude of mind towards the matter ruled by the house in question, while (*b*) and (*c*) denote the circumstances that arise out of it in his particular case. Aspects to the cusp are important if very close. Because they form and dissolve very quickly, they *individualize* the map.

Attention must be paid to the other house ruled by the accidental ruler; such community of rulership connects the two houses and the matters they signify. Thus, in nearly all Libran horoscopes Mars rules the 2nd and the 7th, and thereby shows that the partner will affect the financial conditions more than is ordinarily the case. If Mars were in the 5th, this would be through matters of this house, and so on. Judge from the strength of Mars how this connection would work out.

Again, consider the house ruled by a planet occupying the house under consideration, if there be any. For example, if the 10th house contains the lord of the 6th, and it is much afflicted, judge that the vocation will be affected adversely by health-troubles, bad servants, and so forth.

A conjunction of two planets also unites the affairs of the houses ruled, and, of course, any aspect brings them into mutual relationship according to their nature and that of the aspect. Thus, a planet in the 2nd trine one in the 5th shows gain through speculation; a square, the reverse. These influences are, of course, far from simple, and much experience is needed before one can judge surely; yet, if the student follows astrological teaching, it will not betray his confidence, intricate as many of these rules must seem at first sight.

§ 2. SECONDARY HOUSE INFLUENCES

It is not customary to subdivide the houses into decanates and so on, but one class of sub-influence is of importance.

This arises when considering the affairs of people related to the native, as, for example, the financial affairs of the father. In order to arrive at the correct house we consider the house denoting the relative as his 1st house, and then count from that. Thus the father's money is the 2nd from the 4th, i.e., the 5th, and so on. Again, to judge the wife's health, do not merely consider the 7th, but look at the 12th and 2nd—her 6th and 8th.

It is doubtful, however, if the affairs of others can be detected in this way unless the native is affected by them.

§ 3. HOUSE-ORBS

It is generally considered that an orb of about 5° should be allowed beyond the cusp of each house, and a little more for angles. Some writers advocate extending this to as much as one-third of the preceding house, so that a planet in the last third of a house is considered in the next.

A simpler view seems to be that the houses as such have no orbs, but, as we have seen, the planets have, and thus, if a planet be within 8° or so of a house-cusp it is only natural that its effects will be felt partly through that house, as well as the house it is actually in.

Such positions often seem to link together the two houses in question in a way indicated by the planet. Thus, Mars in the 9th, but near the M.C., might show some loss (δ) of reputation (M.C.) through legal matters (9th).

§ 4. METHODS OF HOUSE-DIVISION
(Beginners are advised to omit this Section)

From very early days astrologers have sought the true method of dividing the mundane sphere into houses and up to the present day there has been more controversy on this topic than upon any other astrological problem. Several systems have been advocated.

Of these the principal are:

(1) The simple "equal house" method attributed, without very clear reasons, to Ptolemy (c. A.D. 70 to 140). See p. 44.

(2) That of Porphyry, a 2nd century Neoplatonist, in which the angles are determined by the horizon and meridian and the sections of the ecliptic between are trisected equally.

(3–4) Those of Campanus and Regiomontanus, in which the angles are similarly determined, but the intermediate cusps are the points whereat the ecliptic is cut by great circles passing from the north and south points of the horizon. In the former system, these divide the prime vertical equally; in the latter, the equator.

Regiomontanus held sway throughout the late middle ages.

(5) Placidus, a mathematician of the 17th century, introduced the semi-arc system, which has been fiercely attacked, chiefly by reason of its failure in high latitudes.

It is to be noted that all these systems, save the first, arrive at the same angles, i.e., cusps of the 1st, 4th, 7th and 10th houses, and only differ in regard to the intermediate cusps.

In the equal method the cusps of the 4th and 10th houses are only identical with the meridian line when 0° Aries or 0° Libra rises; and it must be strongly emphasized that the advocacy of this system by the writer in no wise means that he fails to recognize the immense importance of that line, which indeed no serious astrologer could possibly do. And since it is in mundane square to the horizon, it must have a 4th–10th house significance by analogy; and this must be considered alongside the 4th–10th cusps that are in zodiacal quadrature to the ascendant.

Moreover, as the result of repeated instances of the great strength of bodies placed exactly on the Placidean cusps, especially noticeable in maps cast in the sphere of mundane or political astrology, where the precise time is usually known, the author cannot deny the value of these cusps as lines of power, even if they do not yield such satisfactory results as the Equal Houses method from the point of view of house division.

It should be noted that the principal objection to all these systems except "equal house" is that in high latitudes they become impracticable. For example, in 70° the ascendant and midheaven can coincide in terms of the ecliptic, i.e., the ecliptic can cut the horizon due south.

CHAPTER SIX

THE JUDGMENT OF THE HOROSCOPE: CHARACTER

§ 1

CHARACTER and destiny interact perpetually in life. The man of will and wisdom is able to a large extent to control circumstance. But this is true only of his more mature years; in childhood he necessarily endures the limitations of his environment, and consciously and unconsciously is affected and modified by it, while the ordinary person remains to a large extent the passive recipient of environmental influence throughout his life.

Hence, astrologically, we cannot draw a clear line between that portion of the nativity which works out in terms of character and that which is shown in destiny. In a general sense positions in angles tend to affect the life of physical manifestation, while the succedent houses affect the feelings and character, and the cadent houses the mind. But it will be found that in practice there is an infinite interblending of action, just as there is in real life. If we find a cardinal planet, such as Mars, in a cardinal house and sign, and ruling cardinal houses, then we may be fairly sure that his action will chiefly affect the external life. But such a confluence of planetary action is comparatively rare.

We have already warned the reader against the common statement that "signs affect the 'soul' (or disposition); houses affect the environment (or destiny)". There is no ground for this rule in practical astrology. Saturn afflicted in Leo will show trouble through children just as much as Saturn in the 5th house.

A group of bodies (or *satellitium*) in the 5th house will often produce a very Leo type of temperament, and so on.

In deciding whether a given aspect will work out in terms of character or of destiny the following principles may be of value:

1. So far as character is concerned, contradictory influences tend, as life advances and the character becomes formed, to cancel out.

    Thus in children or childish adults we may find alternate good and bad temper, due perhaps to such contradictory influences as Venus rising in Libra and Moon in Scorpio. But, as the nature becomes stabilized, one or other characteristic, in all probability that which is least compatible with the needs of the environment, will die away.

2. Sidereal influences, when denied manifestation in terms of character, by reason of contradictory indications, then tend to manifest in terms of the external life, such as health, finance, reputation, etc.

    Such action does not seem to be subject to the cancelling-out principle. Thus, if the lord of the 5th were afflicted by the lord of the 2nd, but in good aspect with a planet in that house, then speculative activities would benefit from the one and suffer from the other in separate directions.

It is because of this tendency on the part of aspects to cancel out, so far as character is concerned, that it is impossible to give cut-and-dried accounts of the effects of aspects. Such might be to some extent satisfactory as applied to children or primitive adults, but they would only mislead if referred to men of ideals and progressive moral character.

§ 2. MORAL STATUS

Much has been written on the question: Can the astrologer decide from the horoscope the moral status of the native or must he be informed of this before committing himself to the task of delineation?

Naturally this is a vital consideration, and the answer probably is, that, while he cannot legislate for exceptional cases, for saints or Neros, yet he can as a rule judge the moral condition of the native with considerable accuracy.

For the purpose of discussing this point we can distinguish six classes, corresponding symbolically to the six celestial influences (counting the Lights as the positive and negative sides of the same influence, and omitting ♅, ♆ and ♇).

We must first distinguish two main classes:

1. Those chiefly governed by impulse, instinct, and emotion. These are the Fire-Water types.

2. Those who have reached the deliberative stage, and are governed by definite principles and purposes. These are the Air-Earth types.

Each of these classes may be subdivided as Primitive, Average, and Advanced.

The Primitive Instinctual type is represented by the Brutal Criminal, and the Primitive Deliberative type by the Cunning Criminal. These may be symbolized by Mars and Saturn—of course, in their primitive aspect.

The Average Instinctual type may be represented by the Sun-Moon, and the Average Deliberative by Mercury. It is remarkable how beautifully Astrology, with its recognition of these three influences as morally neutral—neither malefic nor benefic—coincides with this classification.

The Advanced Instinctive type is represented by the person

dominated by generous emotions, i.e., the true philanthropist, symbolized by Jupiter. The Advanced Deliberative type is the true idealist, symbolized by Venus.

It is suggested that Uranus and Neptune may typify the deliberate and instinctive classes, but the natures of these planets are so complex and in some respects anomalous that a decision on this point is difficult.

Reverting to the six types given above, it will be found that a great preponderance in a horoscope of the planetary influences attributed to them will tend to produce persons of the corresponding class. Most persons, of course, belong to the Average category or present a complex of several types.

At best, much Mars and little Venus make the native inclined to roughness and little appreciation of the refinements of life.

Much Saturn and little Jupiter inclines to narrowness, lack of warmth and generosity.

On the other hand, too much Venus and Jupiter make the native too fortunate; he is too well placed in life for his own good, and loses the power of hard work and effort. There is often childishness and irresponsibility, especially with much Libra and Pisces.

Perhaps the best sign of a good moral standard is a strong 9th house. This makes the native conscientious in the best sense, whereas, if the 9th be much afflicted, he often cares little what his actions may be, from the moral point of view.

We may usefully contrast the 5th house with the 9th—the animal impulses with the conscience. The 5th shows what we naturally and instinctively enjoy doing; what we should do, were we unrestrained by moral and social considerations. Thus evil planets here, unchecked by harmonious contacts, may easily have serious results. This is particularly the case with Uranus in the 5th, because of the rebellious and self-willed influence that this planet may exert in a generally ill-controlled horoscope.

The 10th affects us through our sense of self-respect and honour.

The 11th is a friendly, sympathetic house, and bodies well placed therein incline to kindliness and high moral conceptions.

The student must avoid the common mistake of supposing that the mere presence of many "bad" aspects will produce an evil person. This is far from being the case, though such a condition will indicate a difficult life, and, perhaps, many errors of judgment.

The ruler is important. Most criminals have their rulers badly afflicted, and though all who have this horoscopic condition are not criminals, yet their moral character will probably be weak in the direction indicated by the evil influence.[1]

Prominent benefics, especially in relation to the Moon and Mercury, all benefit the nature considerably, and it is usually found that criminals and evil-doers have all four of these bodies severely afflicted. On the other hand, high-principled people may have one or two of them afflicted.

Afflictions to the Sun should be taken as a rule as affecting the *outer life*, and while they may cause the native to make many mistakes and meet frequent misfortunes, they should never by themselves be considered proof of immorality.

Afflictions between Mars and Saturn are often stated in text-books to cause great cruelty, hardness, and even brutality, but this is by no means the case, although, in a bad horoscope, they may augment such characteristics. They are, in fact, quite compatible with sweetness of temper and disposition, but in all cases they seem to destroy the finer side of the Saturn action. The native lacks the real depth of purpose and persis-

---

[1] The reader is cautioned against taking too literally some of the descriptions given in the older style of text-books, themselves often based on older works still, which were written at a time when mankind was more prone to violent self-expression.

Remember to judge the strength of the ruler *by Sign* as well as *Aspect*. A planet in its own positive sign is greatly fortified.

tence of Saturn, and may be superficial or inclined to play at things; or he may live by fits and starts, taking up things and abandoning them again too readily.

A distinction of great importance is that between persons with most bodies in the beginning of the zodiac and those with most bodies in the last signs. This applies particularly to those with many bodies in the *first two* or *last two*. The former class tends to crude and objective expression; the latter to idealistic and subjective attitudes.

Thus the former easily produces a brutal type and the latter a dreamy unpractical one. So the criminal commonly shows many planets in Aries or Taurus and the wastrel many in Aquarius or Pisces.

Here, as in most cases, a good blend is most advantageous. The above refers only to extreme examples.

From an evolutionary standpoint one may say that the Aries-Taurus type is a primitive and at the beginning of his evolution, whilst the Aquarius-Pisces is at the end. But in either case we may get either a good or a faulty expression; the natus shows the stage the ego is at, rather than whether or not it has mastered the lessons of that stage. Each may be good at its own work, and it is certainly pleasanter to see a good expression of the primitive than a defective expression of the evolved.

We now turn to the consideration of the disposition and temperament, apart from the question of the special degree of evolution to which the native has attained.

§ 3. GENERAL DISPOSITION AND TEMPERAMENT

Our first consideration is the *Elements*. We tabulate the number of planets in fire, air, earth, and water signs, and note any preponderance or deficiency. If there appears to be a deficiency, we see if the planetary positions help this. Thus, Sun conj. Mars will to some extent compensate for absence of planets in fire. If there is a marked deficiency or predominance, the effects will be extremely important, and will affect nearly the entire judgment, as, for example, on marriage, vocation, and health. The effects of the elements are given in Chapter Four, and must be carefully studied *from life*. The astrologer must learn to detect the buoyant, self-confident, hearty, or aggressive fire influence; the shrinking, receptive, and yet tenacious water; the plodding, patient, and often commonplace earth; the light, humane, and friendly air. These elemental values are at work in all the objects around us, in our own minds, and in those of others, working in gross or subtle forms, harmoniously or at variance, and their action is the keynote of the Universe.

We now carefully examine the Ascendant, as being the lens through which all influences must pass if they are to be manifest in the life. It is most important that there should be harmony between this and the rest of the horoscope.

If aspects are harmonious, almost any difference can be reconciled, but if the Asc. does not accord with the rest of the map, and this dissimilarity is rendered acute by bad aspects, the resultant conflict is often unfortunate, and the native finds himself at war with himself.

Thus a fire asc. tends to rush headlong into manifestation, and causes acute pain to a sensitive water horoscope, which is thrown into the battle of life against its own inner wish. If the reverse is the case, the timidity of a water Asc. is a great handicap to a fire horoscope, which is continually held back by the sensitiveness of the medium through which it has to manifest.

Fire and earth illustrate a similar discord between enthusiasm and high spirits on the one hand, and commonsense of the other.

Fire and air are less easily antagonized, but may come into conflict in the form of strife between the emotions and the cool, impartial judgment.

Water and air often manifest an acute struggle between the refined humane and intellectual side of the man, and the sensational or even animal side, there being usually a sordid element in the life of primitive water.

Water and earth, being entirely negative, tend in primitive maps to develop selfish and commonplace characteristics; it is an uninspiring and uninspired combination; there is often no great evidence of psychological conflict or disharmony in the nature, because there is too much inertia for even discord to arise.

Air and earth in disharmony show the tension resulting from the difference between the purely intellectual and the practical aims in life. Harmonized, we should have here a man of practical worldly wisdom and also scholarly impartiality and judgment.

Next, the *Qualities*.

Too much cardinality makes the fussy, interfering busybody, unable to let well alone, always trying to manage, and, if there are afflictions in cardinal signs or angles, continually altering his mind and tactics, and giving himself and others much trouble to no purpose. The virtue of the cardinals is their energy and initiative.

Fixed signs predominant, with affliction, show stubbornness and persistence along the wrong lines, ending in disaster. The action of fixed signs is nearly always sudden and far-reaching, but may be held off for years.

If the horoscope is good, we get the man of natural power and authority, occupying a prominent and stable position.

Mutables in affliction cause irresolution, worry, bad temper, nervousness, misunderstandings, and lack of principle. Their virtues lie in their fine mental faculties and adaptability.

The next points to consider are the Rising Sign and its Ruler, any Rising Planet, the Sun, Moon, and Mercury.

The *Rising Sign* relates to the physical body, which is the instrument by which manifestation in the material world is possible. The general characteristics of the signs are given in Chapter Four and those of the planets in Chapter Three. These descriptions will be found to apply when the signs or planets are rising, but attention must also be paid to the *Ruler*, whose importance may easily be overlooked. Much may be learnt as to the character and temperament of the native from this body, as well as of his relations with his environment. The sign and house occupied indicate his tastes and interests as well as how he is placed in life, especially in what may be styled his ordinary everyday life. Further, the aspects to the ruler denote sources of strength and weakness in character and help and hindrance in fortune. For example, if the ruler is square Neptune from the 8th house it denotes constant hindrances from matters of health, a tendency to worry, especially about 8th house matters, and perhaps certain weaknesses of character. But if Jupiter is in good aspect from the 7th, then a close friend or the marriage or business partner will be of a Jovian character and will assist and encourage him to overcome the Neptunian difficulties, and in many ways things and people denoted by Jupiter will befriend and help him, and his own nature will possess Jovian traits that will aid him.

Close aspects to the Rising Degree are important; they influence the natural disposition (as well as the physical qualities) in a marked degree.

A *Rising Planet* often seems to become as it were part-ruler and may be judged as a powerful influence that enters into the native's life and destiny for good or ill, according to its nature and strength by sign and aspect.

Planets on the M.C. are also decidedly important, affecting mainly the fortunes but also the disposition and the ambitions. Some indeed hold that such a planet, if powerful, may virtually become the ruler of the horoscope.

In fact any body in an angular house is powerful, and particularly so if it be exactly on an angle. In such cases benefics unless badly afflicted, are always beneficial in terms of the house occupied, i.e., Venus exactly setting helps the 7th house and is not to be regarded simply as "Venus opposition ascendant"; on the other hand, malefics on the 4th or 7th cusps will be bad for these houses and will probably affect adversely the opposite cusps.

The *Sun and Moon* represent the two poles, positive and negative, of the native's life and energy. The Sun stands for the primal vitalizing principle in the horoscope. In a woman's map its effects are often not very marked, unless she develops a strongly individual life of her own in the world of action. Otherwise they are seen chiefly in the lives of her father and husband. In a man's map it shows where the heart is, where his ambitions and cravings are, especially as regards *doing things*.

The Moon represents the more inner nature, that part of us which seeks to seclude itself, our powers not of giving or doing, but of absorbing and feeling. In a male map its effects often seem to be best seen in the life of the mother or wife.

The Sun is conscious action, the Moon is subconscious. The Sun is deliberate action, the Moon is custom and habit.

The Moon is accumulative, and this quality enables it to store up, digest and assimilate the experiences reaped by the Sun in the field of action. In this aspect, the Moon has much to do with the memory, which is the great accumulation of past experiences.

The Sun tends to denote special and outstanding events and performances; the Moon, habitual characteristics. For instance, Lord Roberts had the Sun trine Mars, and won the V.C. The Moon trine Mars would be more likely to produce the habit of courage on its more negative and passive side, such as patience and endurance.

The Sun and Moon must be most carefully studied, for they are the basis of character and destiny, and their sign- and house-positions repay the most careful attention, as do also their aspects.

Generally speaking, the Moon is the better index of moral character, while the Sun affects the fortunes and achievements of the native.

For example, Sun afflicted by Saturn shows obstacles and a hard struggle in life, but may not affect character perceptibly, while the Moon afflicted by Saturn might denote a timid or hard and mean element in the nature, pronounced or otherwise according to other factors.

In most cases, though not invariably, the lunar position is the most prominent element in the day-to-day behaviour and demeanour; and this is particularly so if the Moon is angular.

Sometimes the solar sign is more clearly marked and sometimes the ascendant or sign of the ruler of the ascendant.

Mercury is the power of self-expression, without which a man may be clever but unable to write or speak freely. While the Sun and Moon are impulsive and instinctive, Mercury is rational, and therefore, if it is strong, it may do much to assist in counteracting other dangerous tendencies. At the same time it is very open to doubt as to whether the position of this planet alone causes moral goodness or depravity, but, since it rules all intellectual expression, its afflictions denote such faults as ill-temper, narrowness or bigotry, carelessness, the tendency to back-bite or criticize harshly, to slander, and so forth. Further, when the general standard of morality is low, an afflicted Mercury lends itself readily to such crimes as forgery, embezzlement, falsification of accounts, and deception of all sorts.

Although this has not been observed by astrologers generally, the 6th house has (as we have already briefly stated) a marked psychological value, indicating as it does to a large extent the moods of the native. This sometimes overrides the ascendant. There seems a noteworthy connection with the native's cheerfulness, or the reverse. Mars afflicted in this house inclines to moody ill-temper; Saturn to taciturnity and unsociableness, a dislike of responsibility, and a pessimistic outlook. The benefics lead to better results, but are nevertheless not strong here.

We now pass to a tabulation of the general effects attributable to planets in signs, bearing in mind that such effects are modified by house and aspect and can really only be considered in the widest sense unless the student has an actual map before him. These effects are most marked in the case of the Sun, Moon, Ruler, and Mercury, but they apply to some extent to all planets.

SUN IN

ARIES	Bold, energetic, generous, stubborn.
TAURUS	Slow, conservative, very fixed.
GEMINI	Quick, changeable, perhaps shallow.
CANCER	Retiring and often a prey to moods; shrewdness and common sense.
LEO	A generous, large-minded, capable nature.
VIRGO	Gentlemanly, accomplished, quiet dignity, hardworking and thorough.
LIBRA	Disputatious, liable to suffer through associates.
SCORPIO	Proud, unyielding, dignified, sometimes overbearing.
SAGITTARIUS	Cheerful, restless, frank, and generous, courteous.
CAPRICORN	Dignified, ambitious, controlled, purposive.
AQUARIUS	Artistic and gifted, peculiar, but sincere and honest; unfortunate through associates unless Sun is strong.
PISCES	Good-natured, kind, hospitable, easy-going.

MOON IN

ARIES	Quick, excitable, pushing, easily roused.
TAURUS	Contented, practical, common-sense, reliable, easy-going, pleasure-loving.
GEMINI	Active mentally and physically, often brilliant, hard, variable.
CANCER	Sensitive, retiring, shrewd, changeful, but sympathetic and protective.
LEO	Kind, affectionate, emotional, fond of pleasure.
VIRGO	Businesslike, and industrious, but often meticulous and fussy; small self-confidence.
LIBRA	Charming, sympathetic, sociable, and happy.

MOON in

SCORPIO	A moody, repressed nature, given to brooding; easily injured and made jealous; often rough and crude; hypercritical.
SAGITTARIUS	Frank, jolly, changeable, and rather superficial.
CAPRICORN	Cold, suspicious, over-cautions, thrifty.
AQUARIUS	Inquisitive, humane, tolerant, friendly.
PISCES	Negative and receptive, easily swayed, kind and affectionate.

MERCURY IN

ARIES	A fiery, disputatious person, easily exaggerates.
TAURUS	Self-opinionated, conventional, limited in interests.
GEMINI	Very quick mentally, fluent, and talkative; dispassionate, rather selfish.
CANCER	Loquacious, emotional, changeable; the memory is good, and there is a tendency to live in the past.
LEO	A firm, determined, rather self-satisfied person.
VIRGO	Neat, quiet, businesslike, and matter-of-fact.
LIBRA	Accomplished, scholarly, social, amusing.
SCORPIO	A deep, silent, repressed person, acute and penetrating.
SAGITTARIUS	Loquacious, shallow, small concentration, careless of detail.
CAPRICORN	Practical, often eloquent and clever; dissatisfied.
AQUARIUS	Scientific, inquisitive, humane.
PISCES	Mentally confused, absent-minded, kindly, often artistic and humorous.

VENUS IN

ARIES	Attractive, but restless, impressionable, and fickle.
TAURUS	Musical, artistic, pleasant, social.
GEMINI	Kind, clever, artistic, gifted in self-expression.
CANCER	Much sympathy, protectiveness, and homely charm.
LEO	Affectionate and warm nature, fond of the good things of life.
VIRGO	Tidy, precise, rather exacting.
LIBRA	Much charm of manner and disposition; a sweet and gentle nature.
SCORPIO	Intense, highly sensitive to neglect or slights; exacting and jealous.
SAGITTARIUS	Affectionate, demonstrative, changeful.
CAPRICORN	Sincere and honourable, conventional, sometimes inclined to snobbishness and worldliness.
AQUARIUS	An idealistic, refined nature; love for the society of friends.
PISCES	Very affectionate, often too easy-going, and easily influenced.

MARS IN

ARIES . . A vigorous, dominant, autocratic nature; unable to compromise or give way; great energy and courage.

TAURUS . . An ill-tempered nature; extreme obstinacy.

GEMINI . . Argumentative, acute, brilliant.

CANCER . . Often moody, quarrelsome, but not courageous; great tenacity.

LEO . . . A powerful personality; generous, hot-tempered, self-willed.

VIRGO . . A good practical worker; thorough and painstaking; apt to be very critical of others.

LIBRA . . Amiable and often charming, but liable to be lazy and easy-going; lacks self-reliance.

SCORPIO . . Strong, dignified, intense and enduring emotions; self-contained.

SAGITTARIUS . Frank, extremely active, full of fun and spirits; apt to be extravagant and over-ready to run after new ideas.

CAPRICORN . A proud, vigorous, decided character, restless, and hates subordination.

AQUARIUS . . Scientific and cultured, high-principled.

PISCES . . Easily played upon by others; emotional, restless, often resentful and discontented.

JUPITER IN

ARIES . . Active, high-spirited, self-willed and liberty-loving.

TAURUS . . Pleasure-loving, indolent, self-indulgent; little inspiration.

GEMINI . . Clever, but often superficial; credulous or sceptical in turn.

CANCER . . Kind, sympathetic, genuine, and good.

LEO . . A magnanimous disposition; full of helpfulness and affection.

VIRGO . . Quiet, critical, kind, but narrow in the affections; matter-of-fact, often conceited.

LIBRA . Good, just, sociable, artistic, or scientific.

SCORPIO . Reserved, dignified, sometimes reckless or self-indulgent; may be conceited.

SAGITTARIUS . A high-spirited, liberty-loving, generous, good-natured person; often reckless; lacking in concentration of effort.

CAPRICORN . Reticent, self-controlled, righteous, and conscientious, sometimes puritanic or austere.

AQUARIUS . . Just, humane, considerate, and often gifted in science.

PISCES . . Jolly, pleasant, easy-going, friendly, and devoted to philanthropy and public work.

SATURN IN

ARIES . . Apt to lack depth; careless and irresponsible; alternately weak and strong.

TAURUS . . Matter-of-fact; may be lethargic, dull, and selfish.

GEMINI . . A serious, profound mind; cold, impartial, and scientific.

CANCER . . A melancholy, repining nature; often clannish, suspicious, mean, and timid.

LEO . . . Reserved, and in some way the nature is stunted, and the feelings denied outlet.

VIRGO . . Careful, practical, conscientious, often severe on others.

LIBRA . . A serious, but pleasant nature, often much spirituality and other-worldliness.

SCORPIO . . Auspicious, proud, restrained, much will-power and endurance.

SAGITTARIUS . Honourable, grave, dignified, often very capable.

CAPRICORN . Able in affairs, materialistic or formal in regard to religion; limited, persistent, careful, and calculating; ambitious.

AQUARIUS . . Scientific, careful, mentally conscientious, humane, exact.

PISCES . . A sad, moody disposition; much sorrow and disappointment; his own enemy.

URANUS IN

ARIES . . Self-willed, proud, extremely courageous, rebellious, vituperative, dogmatic.

TAURUS . . Selfish, immovable, ill-humoured.

GEMINI . . Very gifted, original, and able; inventive and versatile.

CANCER . . Eccentric, very uncertain and strange.

LEO . . . An unfortunate position, often producing uncontrollable emotional storms and hysteria; eccentric.

VIRGO . . Inventive, original, clever, whimsical.

LIBRA . . Romantic, restless, uncertain; often scientific.

SCORPIO . . Concentrated emotions; may be malicious and revengeful, and sensitive to supposed injustice or neglect.

SAGITTARIUS . Rebellious, excitable, highly strung, and reckless.

CAPRICORN . Pushing, restless, dominating, a good organizer and leader, but useless as a servant.

AQUARIUS . . Clever, humane, scientific.

PISCES . . Very unsettled, intermittent, and changeful.

NEPTUNE IN

ARIES . . A schemer, often a subtle, subversive, and dangerous character; in a good horoscope, idealistic.

TAURUS . . Musical, kind, charming.

NEPTUNE in

GEMINI	. .	Fanciful, delicate mentality, often peevish and worrying.
CANCER	. .	Dreamy, mediumistic, lazy.
LEO .	. .	Unreliable, attractive, but weak; inflated idea of own value.
VIRGO	. .	Very critical, and apt to find fault.
LIBRA	. .	Visionary, romantic, subtly attractive.
SCORPIO .	.	Likely to be extremely subtle, and possibly cruel.
SAGITTARIUS	.	Aspiring, visionary, utopian.
CAPRICORN	.	A calculating and scheming character.
AQUARIUS .	.	Much idealism and desire to benefit humanity.
PISCES	. .	Gentle, artistic, and loving; much love of the weak and poor.

NOTE.—It is, of course, impossible to have personal knowledge of people born with Neptune rising in each of the signs, and to a lesser extent this also applies to Uranus. Data from the past are also not always available, and some of the foregoing delineations are therefore, as regards these planets, entirely hypothetical.

It must be borne in mind that the more distant planets stay in the same sign for considerable periods, e.g., Neptune for about 14 years. Hence such placings must refer to whole generations rather than to individuals, unless the planet in question is prominent in the figure.

§ 4. INTELLECTUAL ABILITIES

These cannot be judged from Mercury alone, for this planet rules self-expression rather than actual brainpower. If strong, it nearly always gives fluency with tongue and pen, but it may also be mentally shallow and flippant.

General mental ability seems (in contradiction to the usual belief) to be most clearly indicated by good *solar* aspects, especially to ♂, ♃ or ♅.

Aspects to the asc. affect the brain, regarded as the physical vehicle for mental expression, and weaken and strengthen it according to their nature.

Many bodies in mutables make the mind active, often with a thirst for knowledge, especially the two positives. Virgo may be conservative and conventional. Pisces is artistic rather than strictly mental.

Virgo rising, with a group of planets in Gemini may give a very fine mentality.

The Moon in good aspect to Mercury makes for mental carefulness and soundness. It is an excellent position for a businessman.

Finally, we must mention the 3rd house as frequently affecting the mind very noticeably. Afflictions to it account for most mental affections, such as mental deficiency, dullness, depressions, delusions, morbid fears, and, combined with other heavy afflictions, insanity.

Other things being equal, we may say:

The Sun herein renders the mind strong, self-reliant, and as a rule literary and accomplished.

The Moon causes a dreamy, imaginative, and moody mentality.

Mercury denotes a quick, bright, and witty mind.

Venus improves the disposition, and denotes a kind, courteous, and accomplished mind.

Mars may, if much afflicted, give temper, and indicates an excitable or even hysterical tendency, especially if in water. If strong, there is aptitude for argument and dispute, and the native will more readily perceive differences than agreements between his own ideas and those of others.

Jupiter generally improves the disposition, but detracts somewhat from the purely mental and logical side of the mind. It may show conceit.

Saturn, if strong, gives care, exactness, and conscientiousness to the mental attitude. If weak, there may be melancholy, hardness, narrowness of mental outlook, and even stupidity.

Uranus is well placed as a rule in the 3rd, and gives an original and very active mind.

Neptune, if strong, favours a mystical or artistic character, but when weak may cause much trouble, and inclines to some sort of deception or mental chaos.

These configurations must be collated with the position of Mercury, the accidental ruler of the 3rd, and other significators of character, but their presence can usually be readily detected.

To a less extent these readings will also apply to bodies in the 6th and 8th houses, which often markedly affect the disposition and temper, as already said.

It must be added that very good horoscopical positions are as a rule not so good, nor very bad ones always so bad, as would often at first sight appear, and this applies both to mind and disposition. There seems to be a certain principle of reaction in nature which tends to bring such cases towards the normal.

As an example of this one may cite the natus of the Prince Consort, who was born with Mercury rising in Virgo in major bad aspect with all four malefics from angles. It had no good aspects. Jupiter was almost as weak. The Sun and Moon were in sextile, but had no other good aspects, and only Venus was at all well placed, even she being cadent. The astrologer might easily draw from such a horoscope a gloomy picture, not only of worldly failure, but of mental and moral depravity. Yet the native was a conscientious, enlightened, and accomplished man; he wedded a great monarch, and his married life was certainly far from unhappy. His early unpopularity and premature death seem the chief results of these afflictions.

Afflictions may act as incentives to a powerful and healthy character, whilst "good" configurations may prove temptations to a weak one, inducing it to waste time in self-indulgence and puerilities.

The natus is not, or at least need not be, the Man. It is rather his general life-pattern and the instruments available for his use.

§ 5. THE EFFECTS OF THE ASPECTS[1]

The next consideration is that of the effects of aspects, regarded as influences modifying the planets and so altering their action in respect of character.

[1] These are treated in detail in the author's book *The Astrological Aspects*.

The following notes are studied from life, and should prove helpful to the beginner if read in a wide sense and studied in relation to the more general and deeper psychological issues of the nativity. An attempt to apply them too rigidly, wide as they are, would probably lead to serious misjudgments, apparent if not real. The actual effect delineated might indeed exist in the character, but if overlaid by contrary influences it might easily escape the notice of the native's friends, or even his own, unless he were by training or instinct an acute observer of the inner processes of his mind and feelings.

The notes are based on the permanent, or essential, natures of the heavenly bodies. It is impossible to compile accounts of their influences as differentiated by sign, aspect, and house, for such would run into many thousands. The task, therefore, of adapting each description according to the other factors embodied in each horoscope must be left to the intuition of the student. Astrological delineation is not, and cannot be treated as, a cut-and-dried matter.

The essential natures of the aspecting planets, modified by the signs occupied and the aspects received from other bodies, determine the exact nature of the aspect, which will then seek expression through the houses occupied.

It should be understood that all good aspects tend to bring benefits through the things ruled essentially by the planets in aspect, and trouble if they are in bad aspect. For example, any good aspect to Jupiter will tend to bring benefit through law, foreign affairs, sports, or some other Jovian matter. We must ask the reader to bear this in mind, for it would be a waste of space to repeat it throughout.

The Sun often operates through the father, especially in youth, and, in a woman's horoscope through the husband. Similarly, the Moon stands for the mother, and, in male maps, the wife. Mercury often stands for boys and young people; Venus for young women; Mars for "young middle-aged" men;

Jupiter for those in middle age, and Saturn for the aged. Uranus stand for officials and administrators; Neptune for sailors and artists of all branches of art. Some would relate Pluto to crime and the social underworld, but I should hesitate to endorse such an allocation.

Planets in exaltation or in their own positive signs often perform much good even by bad aspect, especially the benefics, and contrariwise planets debilitated cannot be relied on for great benefits, especially the malefics, whatever aspects they may form.[1]

We must now refer to a point that may already have occurred to the critically minded reader.

If we take an aspect formed between two planets, say Venus and Mars, it will be apparent that by their essential natures these introduce four signs, i.e., in this case, Aries, Taurus, Libra, and Scorpio. They may, however, accidentally rule four houses other than those that correspond to these four signs. They may also occupy yet other signs and houses.

This necessarily introduces, either through planet, sign, or house, a great variety of "influences". In fact in one way or the other almost the entire map may be involved. How then can any clear significance be derived from such a formation?

The answer is that the *essential nature* of the bodies in aspect are predominant. They may be modified by the aspects they receive and by the signs occupied, but Venus is always Venus and Mars always Mars. Saturn may be in trine to Venus, in the sign Leo; but it is still the planet of gravity and austerity.

As for the houses ruled and occupied, these are strictly the fields of operation for the planet and do not modify its action in any other way, unless perhaps very exceptionally indeed. Saturn in the 5th operates through 5th-house affairs, but the fact that the 5th is the house of pleasure does not make Saturn

[1] There is, perhaps, a rather common tendency to place too little importance on sign-position and too much on aspects.

a pleasure-loving planet; rather the effect will be that the native will like serious forms of relaxation, and not frivolous ones.

The sign occupied has a very concrete meaning, despite the common assertion, to which we have already referred, that the signs refer to the disposition. Thus Saturn in Leo often shows disappointment through children. There may be none, or they may be sources of worry and loss.

In Aspect with	THE SUN In Good Aspect	In Bad Aspect
THE MOON	Very wide in effect, benefits business, health, and home. The nature is harmonious.	Generally unfortunate, though in a wide rather than a specific sense. Home-disturbances; the recuperative powers are poor. Heart and digestion may suffer.
MERCURY	The ☌ is thought undesirable by some. The memory is good; some pride and a self-opinionated tendency.	None formed.
VENUS	The ☌ adds to the refinement and artistic ability, but may occasion some degree of affectation and effeminacy.	Only the ∠ is possible. It causes some trouble with the affections. They are too easily stimulated; there may be carelessness and a prodigal tendency.
MARS	A courageous, energetic, and vigorous nature. Success in all matters under the planet. Good for all investigatory work. Often good brain-power, especially with the ✳.	The same, but impetuous, self-willed, extreme emotionally, militant, and even violent. Wastes energy and feelings. Liability to illness or accident under bad directions.
JUPITER	Generous, sincere, honourable, philanthropic, fond of sport, and, in later years, religion or philosophy. A fine testimony to success and health. Prudent yet progressive. Good intellectual powers.	Apt to be involved in unprofitable relations with all Jovian things. May be wasteful, over-hopeful, apt to take risks and lack prudence.

In Aspect with	In Good Aspect	In Bad Aspect
SATURN	Honest, hard-working, careful, persistent, tactful, and ambitious. Gain by steady effort and sober merit. Help from those older and more highly placed.	Many checks and frequent opposition or bad luck. In females usually prevents or much delays marriage and children. Much trouble with old people and those in authority. Misfortunes to the father.
URANUS	An original, energetic mind, dominant and fond of responsibility and leadership; often magnetic and powerful personality. Broadminded; unhampered by convention, drastic.	Clever but perverse, selfwilled and stubborn, often against own interests. Tactless, easily roused to opposition and liable to make many enemies and meet with sudden reverses. Highly strung nerves.
NEPTUNE	Often bestows much good fortune, but affects the character little, except that it may bestow a subtle tendency and love of secrecy.	Loss and worry through confused and treacherous conditions; the native may get himself into bad muddles; he is utopian and unpractical; may be himself irresponsible, foolish, and even tricky.

THE MOON

In Aspect with	In Good Aspect	In Bad Aspect
MERCURY	Greatly quickens and improves the mind; accurate, careful, seldom makes slips. Strengthens brain and nerves.	Clever but careless. A tendency to gossip and backbite. The nerves are often affected.
VENUS	Much affection; a kind, gentle, harmonious, and happy disposition. A happy marriage. Artistic abilities.	Apt to produce slackness, untidiness, and indolence, especially in regard to domestic matters. Affectionate but often silly or childish.
MARS	A quick, practical, decisive temperament; robust and vigorous health.	Rough, and sometimes illtempered or immoral.

In Aspect with	In Good Aspect	In Bad Aspect
JUPITER	Adds greatly to the generosity, sympathy, and warmth of the nature. A truly kind, helpful, and philanthropic nature. Excellent for social and financial advancement.	Trouble through Jovian matters. Careless and extravagant.
SATURN	Thrift, prudence, steadiness, carefulness and perseverance. Cool, self-contained, self-controlled, hard-working.	Great closeness with money, suspicion, timidity, apprehension. Often selfish and narrow. Inefficient.
URANUS	Often gives some psychic ability, such as psychometry, automatic writing. Unexpected benefits.	Nervous troubles. The temper is uncertain, rebellious and resentful; eccentric.
NEPTUNE	Dreamy, imaginative, and bohemian.	Irresponsible, unpractical, muddling; often critical and a fault-finder.

MERCURY

In Aspect with	In Good Aspect	In Bad Aspect
VENUS	The ☌ is one of the best indications of an harmonious, refined, and gentle nature, with a very polished and agreeable manner. Very favourable for artistic work. The ✷ is the same, but less strong.	The ∠ has small effect, but may cause trouble in regard to the things essentially ruled by the planets.
MARS	The mind is sharp, quick, active, able to seize points; a good debater and hard mental worker.	The same, but there is a tendency to be quarrelsome, sarcastic, exaggerative, and careless. There is a danger of mental strain and breakdown. In bad maps, reckless and dishonest.

In Aspect with	In Good Aspect	In Bad Aspect
JUPITER	Prudent, thoughtful, just, and kind; a very understanding mind and good judgment.	Exaggerative, over-optimistic, apt to make mistakes and to be careless about details. Sceptical or superstitious.
SATURN	A quiet, careful, conscientious mind; often a deep and serious turn of thought. Exact and matter-of-fact, logical, and clear.	Narrowness of outlook often hardness and cruelty. Depression. A laborious, pedantic tendency; lack of originality.
URANUS	Clear, original, humorous; brilliant, but often unfitted for routine work; scientific or artistic.	Original, but often eccentric or perverse.
NEPTUNE	Poetic, musical, inspirational; often mystical tendencies; subtle and delicate mind.	Illusive, bohemian, unpractical; often self-deceived.

VENUS

In Aspect with	In Good Aspect	In Bad Aspect
MARS	Feelings and affections are very easily roused, demonstrative; fond of enjoyment.	Separation from the object of the affections; active and sensitive emotions, lack of interior peace and concord; unhappy childhood.
JUPITER	Benefits the social and moral nature, a genial, social person; slight effect on the external life.	Careless, self-indulgent, restless, vain, sometimes revolutionary; often an excess of feeling.
SATURN	Benefits from the aged. Constant and steady affections.	The affections are centred on a very small circle, and are apt to be selfish and exacting. Bereavement and sorrow.
URANUS	Often very attractive and fascinating; artistic and tasteful; romantic.	Romantic, but unfortunate in romance, and often forms attachments of an irregular nature; jealous, uncertain.

In Aspect with	*In Good Aspect*	*In Bad Aspect*
NEPTUNE	A very beautiful and spiritual nature; artistic and poetic. In primitive maps this will have small effect.	Much worry and instability in regard to the affections. Disillusion. The native may have high ideals which are not realized. There may be deception, both in love and finance.

MARS

In Aspect with	*In Good Aspect*	*In Bad Aspect*
JUPITER	Enthusiasm and energy in all Jovian matters; generous and enterprising, but prudent in undertakings.	Wasteful, extravagant, too hopeful; imprudent, often a gambler; may be foolishly enthusiastic about wrong causes; a sectary.
SATURN	A practical, materialistic character, often severe and without appreciation of the finer elements of life.	A hard nature in a bad map; otherwise a lack of true responsibility, inconstancy in carrying out plans. Fitful. Liable to strain and over-work.
URANUS	Physical energy and much muscular strength. A powerful and dominant character.	Often an ungoverned temper. Danger of accidents. A waste of energy.
NEPTUNE	Strong and deep emotions; an unusual power of insight and penetration.	May give suffering from deceit or vice. Obsessions, fears, danger from liquids. Very active imagination.

JUPITER

In Aspect with	*In Good Aspect*	*In Bad Aspect*
SATURN	Steady common-sense and ability; a serious, thoughtful, and stable nature. An excellent augury of enduring success.	Unlucky, lack of enterprise and initiative or else of persistence; narrow or depressing religious views.
URANUS	Great originality, and sometimes mental powers much above the ordinary.	Perverted or misguided ability; dishonesty or rebelliousness; waywardness, lack of self-discipline; many erroneous ideas.

In Aspect with	In Good Aspect	In Bad Aspect
NEPTUNE	Very humane, philanthropic, sympathetic, hospitable and fond of succouring the weak. Spiritual and mystical.	Self-deception or hypocrisy. Indifference to religion, or else superstitious. Very emotional. Undependable unless ♄ is strong.

SATURN

In Aspect with	In Good Aspect	In Bad Aspect
URANUS	A union of will and persistence, common-sense and originality.	The originality is limited for expression or may be perverted into stubbornness and persistence in following wrong tracks.
NEPTUNE	Probably assists much to make the ideals concrete and practical. Common-sense and self-control; powers of organizing. Diplomatic.	The spiritual development is inhibited. Sometimes coldness, cruelty or cynicism. Friends may be deceptive or parasitic.

URANUS

In Aspect with	In Good Aspect	In Bad Aspect
NEPTUNE	Interests in occult and psychic matters.	The same, but a liability to mistakes and delusive beliefs.

IMPORTANT NOTE

Do not forget that too much stress must never be laid on *wide* aspects. It is those that are exact to within a degree or less that really operate vigorously, especially if they fall near a cusp.

CHAPTER SEVEN

THE JUDGMENT OF THE HOROSCOPE.
DESTINY

IN this chapter we must consider, from the twelve houses and the indications affecting them by sign and planet, what the lot of the native is likely to be in respect of health, finance, and other more or less external matters. At the same time we cannot too closely lay to heart that character and destiny are largely inseparable. At times we may believe we have found a temperamental trait that has affected nothing in the outer life, and more often we shall be tempted to say that some event that has befallen ourselves or another "had nothing whatever to do with character". But the more closely we examine such cases the more careful we become of making such assertions.

In some text-books the reader will often find the questions of destiny treated in great detail and at considerable length. The influence of each planet in each house is considered, and often numerous aphorisms, many of them dating from medieval and earlier times, are added. These are of use if read as suggestions, and they often teach the beginner a great deal and may put him on the right track. But so complex is the horoscope that it rarely happens that these descriptions are correct in word and spirit. Mars in the 2nd in Cancer is very different from Mars in 2nd in Leo, and even if it be in the same sign in each of two cases, a trine of Jupiter in one and a square of the Sun in the other may alter the apparent result altogether. *Hence the student should strive above all to master the real meanings or ideas underlying the factors of Astrology and should try to apply them for himself.* He will find many difficult problems, for life is full of complications, paradoxes and surprises;

we understand little of ourselves and less of others. But when he has acquired experience he will find that he can trust Astrology within its proper limits.

§ 1. HEALTH AND DEATH

Physical well-being depends upon the two Luminaries, the asc., and the 6th and 8th houses, as well as, to some extent, the 4th and the 12th. All configurations that involve any of these are liable to affect the health. But if the Lights and rising degree are strong, it will usually be found that such afflictions to the 6th or 8th houses as there may be, or the presence of malefics therein, will not so much cause ill-health or death to the native, as they will cause him distress through others.

The ancient doctrine of the *Hyleg* affirmed that a certain point or body, usually either Sun, Moon, ascendant or Part of Fortune, decided, by its strength of weakness, the length of life; and rules were given to determine which was, in each map, to be taken as hylegiacal.

It is extremely doubtful whether the rule (which appears in various forms) has any value whatever.

The 4th house rules the end of life, and if Venus or Jupiter is therein, or if Saturn (and sometimes Uranus or Neptune) is in strong good aspect to the lord or occupant of this house, it is perhaps as good an indication as any of a long and healthy old age.

It is generally thought that the Sun is most important in a man's map, and the Moon in a woman's, while the latter is always important in childhood, irrespective of sex.

Lunar afflictions often work out largely through wife or mother in a man's nativity, and in a woman's the Sun's aspects often act largely through the father and husband, as we have already said.

The Moon governs the functional health and the Sun the constitution, the complaints resulting from solar afflictions being as a rule more deep-rooted.

If the Sun, Moon, and asc. (the "three hylegiacals") are not badly afflicted, the physical well-being should be assured. The stronger they are the better. Mixed aspects, good and bad, cause varying conditions. If the Luminaries are afflicted in or from angles the results are likely to be the more drastic.

Interplanetary aspects, i.e., not involving ☉, ☽, or cusps of houses, even if involving the 6th and 8th houses, do not usually cause serious trouble unless one or more of these three points be afflicted. Indeed, there is some reason to discount the value of the 6th and 8th from the health standpoint, unless the hylegiacals are involved. But if these latter are aspected from one of these houses, the effects, whether good or evil, will be especially important from the point of view of bodily welfare.

The physical rulerships of the planets are as follows:

THE SUN	General vitality and constitutional strength. The heart and back.
THE MOON	The nutritive and assimilative system. The stomach.
MERCURY	Nerves and respiratory system.
VENUS	Kidneys, throat.
MARS	Muscular and excretory systems. Nose and nasal passages; skull and face.
JUPITER	The blood and liver.
SATURN	The bones, skin.
URANUS AND NEPTUNE	These both work chiefly through the nervous system, but little is known with any certainty as to their physiological rulerships.

Most diseases have been found, by modern astrological research, to be due to the combined action of two or more bodies, so that statements as to a disease being due to one planet or sign are only partially true. It is often found that one hylegiacal is usually afflicted in one disease and another in another, while in one case planetary influence may act by the planet and in another by its sign.

Again, it has been found that many diseases are specially related to certain zodiacal areas, sometimes of a very limited extent. Many of these are published for the first time in the writer's *Encyclopaedia of Psychological Astrology*.

The following traditional sign-rulerships are given subject to the above remarks:

ARIES	.	.	. Head and face.
TAURUS	.	.	. Neck, throat, and larynx.
GEMINI	.	.	. Shoulders, arms, lungs, nervous system.
CANCER	.	.	. Stomach.
LEO .	.	.	. Spine, back, and heart.
VIRGO	.	.	. Bowels and fingers.
LIBRA	.	.	. Kidneys, lumbar region, skin.
SCORPIO	.	.	. Urinary organs and lower bowel, genitals.
SAGITTARIUS	.	.	Hips, thighs, buttocks.
CAPRICORN .	.	.	Bones, knees.
AQUARIUS .	.	.	Ankles. Circulation.
PISCES	.	.	. Feet.

So far as diseases can be ascribed to single planets the following are characteristic maladies:

MERCURY	.	.	. Neurasthenia, epilepsy, nervous excitability.
VENUS	.	.	. Diseases resulting from easy and self-indulgent living. Most forms of kidney trouble.
MARS	.	.	. All feverish conditions, inflammation, sudden, acute, and painful complaints, usually resulting from strain, exhaustion, over-work, or carelessness.
JUPITER	.	.	. Diseases of excess and plethora, such as gout. Abnormal growths. Complaints commonly arise from rich living and need treatment by fasting, hard exercise, and self-denial.
SATURN	.	.	. Diseases are chronic and inhibitive rather than painful (unless Mars is involved as well, as in rheumatic fever). They generally result from poor living, exposure, hardships, or hereditary troubles. Rheumatism is usually shown mainly by an affliction to asc. from this planet. Melancholia.
URANUS	.	.	. Sudden attacks, usually hard to foresee and to cure. The nerves are usually affected. Paralysis is mainly Uranian.
NEPTUNE	.	.	. Extreme physical sensitiveness. Morbid fears, delusions, and other obscure psychic conditions. Liability to nervous worry.

From the standpoint of general vitality the fire signs are reckoned the strongest, although Sagittarius is liable to accidents and Leo is rather commonly occupied hylegiacally in horoscopes of death in infancy. The air signs come next. They are less robust, but they usually lead careful lives, although there is a liability to nervous exhaustion. Among the earthy signs, Virgo is the strongest and often exercises and diets carefully; Taurus tends to be lazy and self-indulgent; Capricorn is often weak as a child, but, once well started, lives long. Scorpio is the strongest of the watery signs, but is very liable to infection, and suffers from bronchial and throat troubles, as well as appendicitis. It, too, is often delicate in infancy. Cancer and Pisces are deemed weak in respect of vitality.

Note that the signs of the 6th and 8th cusps often affect the health, even if no planet is in them. Thus Libra suffers as much from the throat as Taurus, because normally it has this sign on the 8th, and Scorpio seems more liable to bronchitis than Gemini, because it has this sign on the same cusp.

It also happens at times that afflictions seem to work out "by polarity", i.e., through the opposite signs, or even those in square with them. Thus Scorpio is the sign of diphtheria quite as much as is Taurus. All cardinals tend to affect the head, stomach, kidneys, and bones; all fixed signs the throat, heart and trunk, genitals and circulation; and all mutables the nerves, lungs, limbs, and bowels.

The Houses and Health

Generally speaking, the houses have the same values from the physiological standpoint as the corresponding signs, although certain diseases are particularly connected with the former, and others with the latter. For example, mental deficiency and insanity are nearly, if not always, shown by afflictions to the 3rd house, but not necessarily to Gemini, while pneumonia is normally shown by the sign Gemini, and not by the 3rd. Other diseases are particularly planetary. Mercury is often well placed in maps of mental deficiency, but nearly always badly afflicted in insanity. In fact, each disease requires careful study, founded on the examination of sufficiently numerous and reliable instances. Such investigation would add greatly to our understanding both of disease and Astrology.

Infant Mortality

One of the commonest features in the maps of children dead or dying at birth is a malefic exactly on the 4th or 7th cusp in affliction with a hylegiacal, but any affliction to one of these in or from any angle (even if not on the cusp) is critical unless powerful benefic influences intervene. Even then, debilitated benefics (i.e., in fall or detriment, or retrograde) must not be relied upon.

Squares between the 10th and 12th or 4th and 6th are bad, and, if in mutables, the child will have difficulty in establishing respiration.

All three hylegiacals in negative signs seem a common feature of such maps, although Leo often contains one of them.

It is a bad sign if the ruler of the 1st is afflicted in the 8th, or *vice versa*, at least if it is a malefic, but this may by itself only show ill-health.[1]

Moon close to ☌ Sun is considered a weak position, and if a malefic afflict both it is naturally very critical.

Malefics rising are always likely to cause trouble, whereas benefics help to preserve.

Rules given on this matter by ancient writers should be revised in the light of the present-day great fall in the ratio of infant mortality.

---

[1] If it is so placed, but not afflicted at all, it would probably show one much concerned with sickness, as a nurse or doctor.

Death[1]

The time of death is only to be found by a careful study of "directions" (see Chapter Ten), and then not always with certainty, or anything approaching it. Thus, the most extreme care must be observed in giving judgment on this matter, for the responsibility involved is great.

It may be said:

If there be a malefic in the 8th, or one of the Lights badly afflicted, then its arrival by progression to the cusp of that house, and later its reaching the opposition of the asc., are critical periods.

The arrival of any malefic on an angle is a critical period, according to the general tenor of the map.

If the Sun is afflicted by a malefic at birth, its arrival at the next major bad aspect by direction is critical. Thus, if it is square Saturn at birth, it will reach the □ about forty-five years later.

If two malefics mutually afflict, then the arrival of the Sun or asc. at such a place as is in affliction with both at once, marks a dangerous time.

Similarly, many nativities show areas which are under affliction from several bodies radically; such areas are significant of a critical period in the life, should the Sun or asc. have to pass them. The Moon's directions are much less important.

Death is usually denoted by a series of bad directions, without the interposal of any strong good influence, but ⊙ ✳ or △ ♃ is a not infrequent accompaniment of decease, especially of the "happy release" kind.

§ 2. RELATIVES, MARRIAGE, AND FRIENDS

The 3rd, 7th, and 11th houses, corresponding to the three airy signs, are all connected with relationships and show, by

[1] This subject is exhaustively treated in the author's work *Symbolic Directions in Modern Astrology*, Chapter IV.

their rulers and occupants, with what sort of people the native will be brought into contact, and with what results.

The 3rd indicates the brothers and sisters, and, according to some, other near relations. These are, however, best judged as follows:

Aunts and uncles on father's side, as being brethren of the father: 6th;

Aunts and uncles on the mother's side: 12th;

First cousins: the 5th houses from these, i.e., 4th and 10th; and other relations in the same manner. Such judgments cannot, however, be carried very far, and must only be taken to apply to the persons in question in their relation to the native, and not as absolutely true of them as individuals. Otherwise all children of the same parents would have to be born with similar indications in respect of parents, aunts, cousins, etc.

It is probably correct to take the 3rd as denoting especially the eldest brother, the 5th (i.e., third from 3rd) as the second, and the 7th as the third, and so on, omitting those who, by reason of early death or separation, have not influenced the native.[1]

Marriage

Venus and the 7th house stand for unions of all sorts, and especially that of marriage. The children and the procreative instinct are shown by the 5th, and this house also rules court-ship and love-making; so soon, however, as the marriage-tie is formed, whether legally or merely by mutual agreement, the 7th house is the controlling influence.[2]

---

[1] The subject of blood-relationships is a difficult one. Much depends on the nature of the psychological bond between the native and his brothers and sisters. It is obvious that the 3rd cannot indicate all the brothers and sisters, since these will have different, and sometimes very different, nativities.

[2] Tradition has always placed marriage under the 7th house, but the significator of the partner will often be found in the 6th or 8th houses, and it is possible that we have to do with a quadrant, of which the descendant is the centre, rather than with a single house.

In its widest sense it represents all that is complementary to our personal selves (shown by the asc.) all that we lack and seek in others in order to supplement our deficiency. It is the house of all yearnings and seekings after the unattainable or the far distant; the house of the ideal as opposed to the actual, shown by the ascendant.

Astrologically we rarely find two persons born under the same sign to be desirous of marrying one another, and this is readily understandable in the light of what has been said. The ideal, astrologically, is rather that there should be strong points of similarity in the maps of marriage partners, but at the same time points of contrast, in order that each may learn from the other and absorb some of his or her different habits of thoughts and body. Where there is strong similarity and little contrast the couple may often tire of merely being wedded to a counterpart of each other, and even if this does not happen, the lack of contrast may cause the married life to be mentally and emotionally stagnant.

The commonest and strongest tie between a man and woman is probably the presence in the one horoscope of the Sun, Moon, or Venus on the asc. of the other. Such positions occasion very strong physical attraction.

The interchange of the positions of the Lights, i.e., the Sun in one placed on the Moon in the other, makes for deep sympathy and understanding.

Every near correspondence of position in two maps of persons brought into close contact will work out in some way, according to planet, sign, and house.

It is generally said that persons born under signs in square with one another should not marry, owing to the difference of element. This rule cannot by any means be considered absolute, for if the signs in this case are of different elements they are yet of the same quadruplicity. Nevertheless the marriage of two persons with very different preponderances of quality or element is likely to be somewhat risky, although, if successful, it will probably benefit both.

A person who has much fire is likely to wear out emotionally one who is chiefly air, and physically one who is Cancer or Pisces, and so forth.

The general circumstances of the marriage are shown by the 7th house, and by *the application of the appropriate Luminary*. The Sun stands for the male sex in a woman's horoscope, and the Moon for the female in a man's, and the first application of these bodies to radical places denotes the kind of marriage-partner and the conditions of marriage. This often works out with great exactness, the planet to the radical position of which the Light first applies being commonly the ruler or rising planet in the natus of the partner. The theory often propounded, that the successive applications of the luminaries denote successive attachments, and that marriage takes place when, having run the gamut of any bad aspects that it may form, the Light reaches its first good one, must be received with caution.

When the first application of the appropriate Light is to Uranus, Neptune or Pluto, there seems doubt as to what will be the rising sign of the partner, but it seems probable that the planets themselves will in some way be prominent in the partner's map.

This rule can hardly apply in the case of a woman who marries a native of Leo, or of a man who weds a native of Cancer. For obviously the Sun in the one case and the Moon in the other cannot apply to itself. In such instances the appropriate Luminary will probably be found to apply to a planet strong in the partner's map but not, of course, ruling the rising sign. Often it is the dispositor of the Sun.

If the Luminary appropriate to the case applies by good aspect to a planet, it is probable that marriage will take place readily to a person denoted by that body, whatever subsequent applications may be made. If it applies to a benefic or neutral by square or opposition, marriage will probably ensue, but will be attended by some trouble, as shown by sign and house. If the application be by bad aspect to a malefic, either no marriage or an unhappy one must be expected. Saturn is more likely to deny or greatly delay marriage, Mars or Uranus to hurry it with regrettable consequence, Neptune denotes strange, unaccountable conditions.

The 7th house has a wide significance, embracing all partnerships or relationships between the native and individuals. It is possible that the general conditions of marriage are shown by this house, and that the application of the Luminary has more to do with the actual wooing and events immediately subsequent to marriage.

The following are the probable results of the presence of the planets or lights in the 7th, and the same is to some extent true of their aspects to its ruler:

THE SUN . . .	A proud, firm-minded partner, with much personality. In the case of women's maps, this delays marriage.
THE MOON . .	A kind, domesticated partner, but often much change of moods and feelings on both sides.
MERCURY . . .	A quick-minded, intellectual partner, or, if afflicted, a bad-tempered, critical, or nagging one.
VENUS . . .	The marriage is likely to be happy, and the relations between the partners affectionate and a source of joy to each.
MARS . . .	A strong-minded, and domineering partner. Likelihood of frequent separation, either by quarrels or force of circumstances.
JUPITER . . .	Prosperity is likely to come through marriage, but it is not always found that this position favours happiness. There is often death and a second marriage.
SATURN . . .	Difference of age or station between native and partner. Marriage is late. The partner is likely to be faithful, but often cold or worldly, and engaged on professional considerations to the neglect of wife and home. Narrow affections.

URANUS . . . Romantic or tragic conditions in wedlock, according to aspects. The planet is too freedom-loving and forceful to favour happiness in marriage unless aspects are very good. Generally an undesirable significator, unless unusual and unconventional experiences are sought.

NEPTUNE . . . Like Uranus, often causes highly unexpected and mysterious events in marriage. Danger of deception, instability, or, in a map of an advanced kind, there may be a platonic union, or one arising from some other form of idealism. Often causes marriage to a cripple or person in some way deformed or injured.

Both Uranus and Neptune incline to extreme sensitiveness, which in itself does not assist towards connubial happiness.

It is necessary to distinguish between positions causing ill-fortune in marriage and those causing unhappiness and dis-agreement. In allying oneself closely to another, one assumes, to some extent, their nativities and the good and evil therein, and the closer the union the truer this is. Hence it not infre-quently happens that marriage is followed by an abrupt change of "luck", not always explicable in the light of ordinary common-sense. Parts of a natus that have lain dormant may be suddenly stimulated into action. If, for example, a man marries a woman with the Sun applying to the square of Uranus, any element in his horoscope that threatens sudden illness or accidents will be likely to come into action.

On the other hand, happiness in marriage from the emotional standpoint depends on the general suitability of the two horo-scopes, their special points of correspondence as explained above, and perhaps more than anything else on Venus. If this is well aspected, especially by the Moon, happiness is probable, irrespective of what the marriage may bring in the way of material trials.

If, however, Venus be afflicted by Mars we are likely to find tumultuous feelings and little emotional calm or happiness, with prolonged separation; if by Jupiter, extravagance of feeling, and often lack of sincerity and a restlessness that may easily lead to infidelity; if by Saturn, jealousy, despondency, and ingratitude; if by Uranus, an uncontrollable craving for romance and adventures; if by Neptune, unattainable ideals and consequent unhappiness.

The physical side of marriage comes mainly under the 5th house, and this house also has a good deal to do with the emotions generally. The lord of the 7th in 5th, or *vice versa*, usually shows a love-marriage, or at least one that is not the result of worldly motives. Good aspects between the lords of the houses indicate that marital happiness will be augmented by the physical side of marriage; and conversely. Heavy bad aspects between 5th and 7th, especially of Saturn, may denote lifelong celibacy. The appropriate luminary applying closely to the bad aspects of Saturn often indicates the same, whereas similar applications to Mars may denote a difficulty in controlling the passions.

With regard to cases where the appropriate luminary separates from an aspect, it is usually the case that this does not cause marriage, but denotes abortive attachments, pleasant or otherwise, according to the nature of the aspect.

The signs, when ascending, tend in varying degrees to produce characteristic fortunes in marriage.

Aries is usually impetuous, warm in feelings, but apt to make a self-willed and obstinate partner. It marries in haste, and probably often repents at leisure.

Taurus rising places Scorpio on the 7th, and this generally causes some danger of illness or death to the partner, and, if not these, at least some form of separation, such as may be due to military or naval service.

Gemini, having Sagittarius on the 7th, often has double attachments or two marriages, or marriage to a foreigner, or one connected with a Jovian occupation. It is often a hardened coquette or philanderer, and is rarely carried away by its feelings.

Cancer is usually a faithful, affectionate, and devoted husband or wife; there is often a tendency in Cancerian women to marry those who owing to youth or incapacity need "mothering".

Leo is notoriously often unhappy in marriage, despite its warmness of heart and frequent unselfishness.

Virgo, having Pisces on the 7th, nearly always passes through worry and confusion in its love-affairs, frequently becoming involved in some scandal or other trouble. As a partner it is generally faithful and attentive. It rarely marries very early.

Libra is easy-going and readily satisfied; it takes its emotional adventures calmly, and, although lacking intensity of affection, is easy to live with.

Scorpio has extremely deep and intense feelings; is liable to jealousy, and although devoted, is often exacting.

Sagittarius generally has several love-affairs, and often two marriages. The feelings are warm but changeful, and without true sympathy or understanding.

Capricorn is little suited to domesticity, and may marry for social reasons or professional ambition, or otherwise subordinate the home-life to the vocational.

Aquarius, although its code of sexual morality is usually its own, so that it is often unconventional and romantic, frequently turns into an affectionate and sincere partner when once settled in life.

Pisces seems more liable than any sign to plural marriages.

Non-marriage is generally shown by the appropriate luminary making no application at all, and the absence of planets in the 7th house. ♄ afflicting the appropriate luminary or the lord of the 5th may show celibacy.

Indeed, such configurations tend to denote a life into which relations with the other sex hardly enter at all, whereas malefics in the 7th badly afflicted show trouble in such matters.

If the luminary leaves bad aspects of the malefics it also denies marriage, whereas if it applies to such, marriage may take place, or there will at least be love-affairs, but disagreement, estrangement, sickness, or death are likely.

Traditionally marriage is considered much more likely if significators are in the so-called "fruitful" signs, which are the same as the watery trigon. Several rules have indeed been handed down by tradition relative to late and early marriage, as well as numerous aphorisms on sexual matters, but the student is advised to accept these cautiously. They are often interesting, but a clear grasp of principles is of far greater value than a knowledge of any number of isolated rules, exact parallels to which it is difficult to find.

Certain zodiacal areas are found, for reasons not yet understood, to be specially indicative of trouble in marriage and sex-relations generally, if involved in afflictions or occupied by malefics. Thus, 8° Aries-Libra, 25° Virgo, 19° Leo-Aquarius, and 27° Leo-Aquarius.

Horoscopes erected for the time of marriage are often indicative of the subsequent course of wedded life.

Friends

As the 5th shows our personal pleasures, so the 11th shows our mental interests, our wishes, hopes, and aspirations, and our friendships.

This house may be judged from the bodies ruling or occupying it, and from these we can form an opinion as to the kinds of friendships the native will make and the course that such friendships will follow, as well as the influence that these will have upon his life.

If the lord 11th be in good aspect with the ruler of the horoscope it shows harmonious relationships with friends; if it be in good aspect with the planet in or ruling the 10th, it shows help from friends and so on.

All clubs, societies, and associations come under the 11th.

§ 3. VOCATION AND FINANCE

Vocation may be judged in a general sense from the whole horoscope and the type of person whom it represents.

Thus a cardinal person needs an active outlet for energy and scope for initiative. A fixed individual will do better in a settled position, with a routine that requires judgment and decision, but not great push or enterprise. A mutable person will do best in a clerical or academic capacity.

In the same way, fire inclines to outdoor occupations; air, to mental ones; water, to the sea, the liquor trade, and many every-day occupations; earth, to agriculture, farming, stock-raising.

The signs have each their special affinities in the world of business and profession:

ARIES . . .		Engineering, soldiering.
TAURUS . . .		Farming, stock-breeding, cashiers and those who handle hard cash, music.
GEMINI . . .		Journalism, writing, driving vehicles for hire, teaching, Post Office, printing.
CANCER . . .		Trade of all sorts and shopkeeping, especially in household commodities; boating and shipping.
LEO		Stock Exchange, finance, company promoting; management and control of many kinds, especially in connection with amusements, such as cinemas and the stage.
VIRGO . . .		Clerical and secretarial; medicine, gardening, physical culture, writing.
LIBRA . . .		Jewellery, millinery, dress, wine-trade; often go to sea, brokers and agents of all sorts.
SCORPIO . . .		Surgeons, sanitary inspectors, chemists, soldiers and sailors, undertakers, butchers, analysts.
SAGITTARIUS . .		Religion and the law, professional athletes, publishing, exploration.
CAPRICORN . . .		Politics, mining, managerial posts of many kinds, Government employ, labour exchange officials.
AQUARIUS . . .		Many intellectual pursuits, such as teaching and lecturing, music and science.

PISCES   .   .   .   Trades connected with cloth and wool, grocery, footwear sale and manufacture, the sea, plumbing, the drama, hotels, inns, liquor, painting, welfare work, charities, nursing, the Church.

It must be borne in mind that these influences affect the native's personal inclinations when the sign in question is rising, but the signs may also potently affect the destiny by being on one or more of the three "earthy" houses. It is in this way that people find themselves forced or drifting into an uncongenial occupation; the asc. indicates their natural inclination, but some strong sign or planetary position on the 2nd, 6th, or 10th places them in another walk of life altogether. As, for example, a man with Mars and Jupiter rising in Scorpio is made for an open-air life, and would be perfectly at home "roughing it", but he has Mercury in Virgo on the M.C., and destiny decrees that he must go into a city office, until the force of character shown by the rising sign and planets can assert itself.

Such cases as these are not uncommon, especially when people are born with strong planets in the 12th. Their early life is obscure and their conditions distasteful, but as the planets by progression[1] pass into the 11th and 10th their personal ideals overcome the obstacles denoted by their natal 10th and 4th houses.

When the significators of character are harmoniously placed as regards the vocational houses, a person will find his right path in life.

Great attention should be paid to the strongest planet, for this denotes the category of things most beneficial to the native and most congenial to his own nature. *A strong solar aspect is always very important. Do not overlook the ruler.*

As regards wealth and success, property, as such, comes under

[1] See Chapter Ten.

Saturn and most propertied people have this planet either angular, or in aspect to the Sun, or, better still, both. Even bad aspects from Saturn to the Sun are not inconsistent with financial success; but in this case it will be limited and there will always be danger of loss; moreover, the position will entail heavy responsibilities.

Venus gives success through the help of others and from personal charm.

Jupiter gives success through good fortune; and this planet angular, or configured with the Sun, favours success. However, the planet, of itself, does not accumulate, and, if afflicted, indicates loss through over-optimism, gambling, hazardous enterprises, and inordinate generosity. Investments abroad are not likely to succeed and lawsuits should be avoided.

Mars gives fortune by effort; his good aspects show gain through pluck and hard work.

On the other hand, when much afflicted, he may show hard times of a very bitter sort. Mars, however, has not such a depressing effect as Saturn, and his influence does not seem so interminable or so insuperable. Generally he spends and earns freely, like all fire, while Saturn works slowly and methodically and saves carefully.

Uranian aspects tend to give trouble or benefit as the case may be through government and officials. The native often likes responsibility, and will shoulder it to any extent rather than remain in the background, or be obliged to defer to others, or seek favour with them, or use tact and persuasion. A prominent afflicted Uranus is likely to make any sort of worldly success almost impossible, since the native will be wilful, uncertain in temper, impatient, and perverse.

Neptune, by good aspect, sometimes produces much good fortune, but this has the reputation of being of the nature, often enough, of "fairy gold", with little substance behind it. It favours success by the sea and, generally, in ♓ occupations (see list above). In bad aspect it occasions worry, trickery, and impracticable schemes.

A careful scrutiny of the 2nd house and the aspects it receives will generally reveal the native's fortune in regard to finance, the good aspects showing whence money will come, and the evil where it will be lost.

The 5th rules speculation, and if this is afflicted, especially in regard to the 2nd, all risky finance should be avoided. Unusual success in speculation is generally denoted by strong good Uranian aspects to the 5th, but even if these are found in the map, they should not be strained too far.

The 6th is important since it shows what sort of servants the native will have, and whether they will serve him well or dishonestly, and what sorts of faults they will be most prone to commit.

The 7th is involved in all questions of partnership and all kinds of "deals" or negotiations. Hence its value in nearly all business transactions.

The 8th rules all legacies, as well as the partner's money. Thus an affliction between 2nd and 8th would lead to disputes between partners as to money, or loss to one through the finances of the other.

The 10th denotes the social and financial ambitions, which may or may not be realized. It indicates what sort of a figure the native wishes to cut in the world, or, if afflicted, the figure he will have to cut whether he wish to do so or not. It may also denote parental conditions. It is subserved by the two other occupational houses, representing finance and work, both of which unite to produce that which is denoted by the 10th, i.e., status.

Near the meridian the three fire bodies—Sun, Mars, and Jupiter—all give pride which may incline to arrogance. They tend to a keen sense of personal honour, and, especially in fixed signs, family honour as well. They attract respect.

Mercury on the M.C. tends to make the native pliable and adaptable, and Venus popular, kindly, and good-natured. Neither planet can be considered strong on the meridian, except in so far as a prominent Venus is always better than a weak one.

These characteristics may affect the selection of the vocation and success therein.

Saturn on the M.C. is a critical position. It gives responsibility, and, as a rule, ambition of a persistent kind. If strong it may denote success by merit and perseverance, but it seems liable, if in any way afflicted, to cause ultimate reverses and even downfall. It may denote a similar fate for the father. Saturn weak on M.C. is very likely to indicate a worldly and over-economical parent, and his financial misfortune in old age, especially if it be in Cancer, or afflict the Moon.

Uranus on the M.C. shows many changes of occupation. It inclines either to some unusual scientific profession, such as research, or else to official positions. In any case, the native usually aims at independence of control, and uses original methods. Under affliction the planet may show heavy misfortunes.

Neptune in the 10th exposes the native to scandal and misrepresentation. It causes the ambitions of the native to be idealistic and unselfish in a good horoscope. In a bad, the imagination may run wild, and the native will involve himself and others in a morass of muddle and illusion. It does not seem to influence the choice of vocation greatly, however much it may affect the native's conduct in the same.

The Part of Fortune is considered by some to have great influence on wealth. This matter has been already discussed (see page 30), and the opinion expressed that such is by no means necessarily the case. It is rather an important centre of self-expression, and necessarily becomes significant of finance in the horoscopes of those whose activities are to a predominant extent directed towards monetary matters.

This is not the place to discuss such a subject as Investment. We may say that several branches of Astrology apply here; but the most important point is to decide what planet or planets is most strongly configured with the 2nd house and, having done so, to use this planet as an indicator of the markets and countries most favourable to the native in question. For example, Mercury might indicate newspapers and paper-manufacturing firms, especially if they had connections with a Mercury country such as Wales or U.S.A.

The registration-maps of public companies may also be compared with the nativity under review.

§ 4. ACCIDENTS AND VIOLENT DEATHS

Liability to accidents is not easily distinguished from liability to disease, and frequently the same aspect will, at different times, denote both.

It may be said that the former are caused by severe afflictions to the hylegiacal points from the malefics Mars, Saturn, and Uranus, especially, perhaps, the first. They are said to be especially likely to cause accidents when on the east side of the map, and when angular and cardinal, but it is doubtful if too much attention should be paid to this, for it is obvious that accidents are capable of considerable differentiation according to their cause (whether the native's fault or otherwise), and according to their special natures. One would expect accidents due to carelessness or lack of foresight or agility to be due to mutable afflictions quite as much as to aspects in cardinals.

Generally speaking, it seems that afflictions from the last few degrees of cardinals are especially likely to cause accidents, but I believe that nativities of victims of accidents are usually characterized by a special prominence of the ends of mutable signs as well. Bodies forming no aspect before leaving the sign they are in are termed "void of course", and possibly such positions favour accidents.

Mars causes burns, stabbing, cuts, shooting.

Saturn: falls, blows, collisions, and crushing.

Uranus: explosions, electrocution, and accidents with machinery.

Mars or Uranus in conjunction or opposition to a hylegiacal point are common indications of accidents of a severe kind; squares seem less common.

The four signs ruled by Mars and Saturn, and also Libra, are said to cause violence.

In all cases observe the severity of the affliction and consider how far the benefics may be expected to mitigate it.

Drowning is specially shown by afflictions involving the end of Gemini and Sagittarius, or beginnings of Cancer-Capricorn; and the end of Aries-Libra and begining of Taurus-Scorpio.

Murdered persons' nativities generally show violent afflictions in one or more of the following areas: beginnings of the cardinals, about 17° of the cardinals, and the end of the fixed signs (less common).

Those suffering death by judicial sentence generally have a planet (particularly Jupiter) in 17° of the mutables.

Suicides usually have Uranus severely afflicting, especially Mars. Jupiter is generally weak; there are often few planets in cardinal signs. Mercury and the 3rd are generally afflicted, and common zodiacal areas are 25° of the fixed and about 26° of the mutables.

Poison is connected with Virgo and Scorpio, and Mars and Neptune, while 12° Virgo-Pisces and 11° of the cardinals are common zodiacal areas.

Danger from fire, whether to the person or to property, is often indicated by Mars-Saturn afflictions.

Death in battle is commonly shown by a marked Saturnian element, as well as Martian, and violent afflictions in or near 12° of the mutables are frequent.

Other kinds of violent death must be studied in the light of general principles applied to each special case. Our knowledge on these matters is in its infancy, but we have reason to believe that, with the growth of scientific astrological investigation, based on statistical research, it is destined in time to become far more precise and reliable.[1]

§ 5. Parents and Children

The 4th is taken to indicate the father and the 10th the mother, but this allocation has been questioned on the grounds that the Moon, natural ruler of the 4th, is said to signify the mother, and the 10th, corresponding to Capricorn ruled by Saturn, the natural significator of the aged and those in authority, suggests the father.

By some the Moon by night and Venus by day are said to indicate the mother, and similarly the Sun by day and Saturn by night the father. It is possible that none of these bodies definitely stands for either parent. The Moon signifies women generally, and in particular mother and wife, while the Sun stands for men in general, and father and husband in particular, and Saturn is representative of age and authority. The 4th house is the home, and the 10th the public status, and these depend to a large extent, in early life, on the mother and father respectively.

Malefics in the 4th and 10th certainly affect the parents. An opposition between these houses or a bad aspect between the rulers often shows parental disagreement or separation.

The Sun afflicted by Saturn often brings trouble to the father, and, through him, to the native; there may be long illness, business misfortunes, or bankruptcy; or it may show a cold, severe father.

---

[1] This subject is treated in detail in the author's *Astrology of Accidents*.

The Moon so afflicted often makes the mother mean, melancholy, selfish, or hard, or merely unfortunate and unable to help the native. On the other hand, benefics with the luminaries or in the two houses bring help through the parents. Indeed, in early life both Sun, Moon and the 4th and 10th operate largely by way of the parents.

Afflictions to the luminaries from Mars threaten the parents with accidents, illness of a Martian type, or immorality. From Jupiter, wastefulness and extravagance. From Uranus, their sudden downfall, or at times insanity. From Neptune, their downfall through muddle or trickery or, sometimes, drink.

The parents' affairs may to a large extent be judged by taking the appropriate house as their 1st, and then proceeding as explained on page 89.

Children are denoted by the 5th, and, to some extent, by the 11th, which is the 5th from the 7th, and so denotes the partner's children.[1] As regards their number, the watery signs are considered most prolific, or "fruitful", and the fiery (with the possible exception of Sagittarius) and Capricorn the most sterile. The airy signs are average in this respect. Taurus is more fruitful than Virgo, and is moderately prolific.

Among the planets the benefics, the Moon, and perhaps Neptune are prolific; the Sun, Mars, Saturn, and Uranus, barren, and the last-named inclines to artificial prevention of conception. Mercury is probably barren, though much influenced by the sign occupied and aspects.

Twins are usually shown by significators in double signs, i.e., Gemini, Sagittarius, and Pisces.

Attention should be paid to planets in the 5th, the sign on the cusp, the position of the Moon, and, in women's maps, the Sun also, while in all cases the ascending sign is important.

---

[1] Such is the traditional teaching. But I have found that the 12th, its ruler and the planets therein are better indices of the children, or, at least, of the eldest. Thus Libra often has Virgo children, and so on.

The traditional effects of the planets in the 5th may in a general sense be described as follows:

The *Sun*—few children, but possibility of one being famous or successful.

The *Moon*—increases the number; they are likely to be commonplace or ordinary in character, unless there are brilliant aspects.

Mercury—clever and intellectual children; if afflicted, worry through them.

Venus—gifted and affectionate children, and much pleasure through them. They are likely to be well-favoured and popular.

Mars—turbulent and self-willed children; they are few in number, and are likely to suffer from accidents, if the planet is afflicted. If it has a square from the 8th, danger of their sickness. Separation from children.

Jupiter—prosperous and respectable children, often good at sports.

Saturn—few children, and they are often sickly or unfortunate; the native feels the responsibility of parenthood heavily; there may be coldness or estrangement between parent and child.

Uranus—eccentric or talented children; this planet in the 5th does not favour many children.

Neptune—gives a morbid hatred of children in some cases, and in others an ungratified desire for them. They will be dreamy or artistic.

The signs when ascending have special effects as regards children, due to the nature of the sign then falling on the 5th. Thus, Librans usually make friends of their children, because Aquarius is generally on the 5th when Libra rises, and so on. These secondary influences are often well marked, and the student should exercise his intuition in discovering them for himself.

The sex of the children is judged from the nature of the

signs on the 5th, occupied by the ruler of that house, and containing the Moon. Positive (odd) signs are considered masculine; negative (even) are deemed feminine. In the same way Moon, Venus, and Neptune incline to female children, and the other planets to masculine, except Mercury, which alters according to sign and aspect.

Traditional astrology places great stress on the 5th house in regard to children, but my own experience is that, whilst this house certainly does frequently indicate the dispositions of the children, their liability to illness and accidents, and so forth, the question of the *number* of children depends more upon the Sun (in women) and the Moon (in men). Afflictions to these bodies from Saturn often show childlessness.

Sun afflicted by Uranus in female maps denotes danger of miscarriage.

In some families there are marked similarities in the maps of the members, aspects and sign-positions recurring frequently. For example, Mercury in 4th may show a constant appearance of Gemini or Virgo values. But in other cases, presumably where the family-ties are relatively loose, there are hardly any such repetitions.

§ 6. TRAVEL

This is connected mainly with the 3rd house, governing short journeys, and the 9th, governing long ones. The distinction usually drawn is that the 3rd rules all journeys that may be completed within the day; the 9th all longer ones. But it is suggested that the real distinction lies rather in the nature of the journey, the 3rd denoting routine travelling, and the 9th those that bring one into contact with new conditions, partaking to some extent of exploration.

Cardinal and mutable signs incline to travel, and so do the planets Mercury and Jupiter, and the Moon. Fixed signs are the reverse, and if these preponderate, especially in respect of the lords of the two houses mentioned, there will be little love of change of abode.

Many planets in Cancer or the 4th give a love of home, and yet there is usually a good deal of moving about in connection with business. The Moon in the vocational houses (2nd, 6th, and 10th) inclines to business journeys. If she rises the same is often the case, and the ruler of the horoscope in the 3rd or 9th, or the rulers of these in the 1st, all tend to bring travel into the life.

The fiery signs all like to get about and see life, especially Sagittarius, and both Libra and Pisces seem often to be wanderers in a physical sense, as well as mentally and emotionally.

A strong 9th, as by benefics or Sun and Moon well aspected being therein, or the ruler strong, makes travelling profitable, and may lead to success abroad, and, if in addition to this, malefics afflict the 4th, the native should leave home and seek a country ruled by the planets strongest in regard to the 9th house and generally.

It is traditionally believed that success may be obtained by settling in a place where one of the benefics at the time of birth was on an angle. Similarly malefics may be removed from awkward positions.

A careful study of the aspects received by the ruler of the 9th and any planet that may be in it will show the results of travel. Thus a good aspect from the 2nd would show pecuniary benefit, from the 6th benefit to the health, and from the 5th pleasure and enjoyment.

§ 7. RELIGION, MYSTICISM, AND OCCULTISM

Religion and philosophy come under the 9th house, which denotes the mind in its most expansive and explorative aspect, seeking to fathom life's mysteries intellectually. At the same time, since it corresponds to a fiery sign, it possesses faith and hope when manifesting harmoniously.

The Sun in the 9th inclines, generally, to fixed ideas, and it may denote positions of importance in regard to the Churches, but its influence on religious thought depends mainly on aspects and sign.

The Moon inclines to psychic experiences, queer dreams, and, in a weak map, superstitions and vulgar prejudices.

Mercury causes an active, inquiring and sceptical mind, sometimes superficial and flippant. Much depends on aspects.

Venus makes for a poetic or artistic faith with a love of beautiful ceremonies and musical worship.

Mars may cause the native to be a bigot, either on the side of religion or against it, or the native may be completely indifferent.

Jupiter denotes a truly pious, reverent, and philanthropic nature, although bad afflictions may cause formalism, hypocrisy, or a conventional outlook.

Saturn, if strong in this house, makes for profound thought, being intellectual rather than emotional, and favouring either an austere puritanic religion, or a severe philosophy, such as Stoicism. If weak, there is religious depression and fears, fatalism, or hopeless agnosticism.

Uranus here may make an original and profound thinker, or, afflicted, an eccentric.

Neptune inclines to such beliefs as Christian Science, spiritualism, or some form of mysticism.

Fiery signs incline, when on the 9th, to religious emotion; airy to philosophy and metaphysics; water to occultism on the one hand, or foolish superstition on the other; earth is often indifferent or formal.

The three houses corresponding to the water trigon rule the hidden, withdrawn side of nature, and many planets therein nearly always incline to some form of occultism, varying in quality, of course, with the general character of the native and the opportunites encountered for rational instruction in such matters. We may thus get abject superstition or profound insight and knowledge.

Uranus and Neptune possess special importance in all horoscopes which we desire to study from the standpoint of occultism, and if these are severely afflicted, much caution must be exercised in regard to such matters, and instruction should only be accepted from teachers of established good faith and recognized sanity of outlook. Otherwise much time and energy will be wasted at the best, and at the worst the native may easily suffer lasting injury, mentally, emotionally, or physically, as the case may be.

Occultly the influence of Neptune is far more subtle and intangible than that of Uranus, which seems to deal with definite and understandable facts and laws, whereas Neptune induces states of consciousness that possess values beyond earthly measurement, but at the same time are fleeting and not to be constrained.

Astrology has so many sides and there are so many avenues of approach to it, that it can hardly be said that there is a characteristic astrologer's nativity. It appears to come largely under the 9th house in its philosophic and also in its prognostic aspects, for Sagittarius is the sign of prophecy. It is also largely Saturnian, on the positive Aquarian side, while Uranus is considered specially the planet of the astrologer. Strong aspects between the Sun and Neptune also occur in the genitures of many famous astrologers, especially the ☌ or parallel of declination.

It is very common to find planets—especially the Moon, Venus, or Saturn—in or near 27° Leo-Aquarius in the horoscopes of astrologers, and to a lesser extent in or near 11° Virgo-Pisces.

CHAPTER EIGHT

TWO EXAMPLES OF DELINEATION

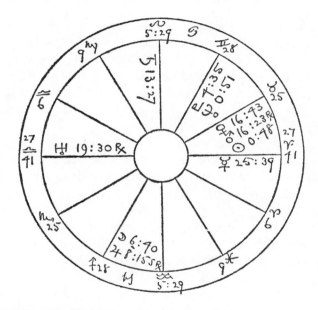

ABOVE we give the Natus of Adolf Hitler.[1]

Authenticity of Data.—This should always be the first consideration and the student should make a careful note on all his maps on this point.

The recorded time was 6 hrs. 30 mins. p.m., April 20, 1889, at Braunau. This would be equivalent to 6 hrs. 22 mins. true

[1] In earlier editions the natus of Queen Elizabeth I was given, but this labours under the drawback of an uncertain birth-time, research inclining strongly to a Capricorn ascendant. It has been thought better to substitute a more modern horoscope.

local time, for Braunau is 2° west of the Central European meridian. On the Continent the time of birth is recorded by the attendant physician, but usually only approximately, and we have allowed ourselves a slight alteration for reasons based on the pre-natal epoch. But this will not materially affect what we shall have to say.

Character.—The ruler, Venus, is in its own negative sign, but is in very close conjunction with Mars, which is in its negative detriment, and both bodies are in square to Saturn; this planet is obviously very strong in the sense that it is near the mid-heaven and disposes of both Moon and Jupiter. But it is in detriment in Leo and its only good aspect is a quintile to Neptune.

The Moon is in detriment and Jupiter is in fall, but they are in close conjunction in the house of the lower mind. They cannot be said to have any important aspects; indeed the only contacts are a wide trine to the Sun, and biquintiles to Neptune, the value of which is rather a moot-point.

The ascending degree has also a curious isolation. Uranus has risen and stands between the cusp of the 1st and the latter part of the 12th house, a condition that tends to the neurotic, as seems not unnatural, when one bears in mind the values of the planet and houses concerned. Mercury, too, opposes the ascendant, as does the Sun; indeed, if our rectification is correct, the opposite point to the ascendant falls just between Sun and Mercury. Thus the ascendant is not strongly aspected at all, and what contacts it makes are significant of poor mental balance. We may make one exception to this: there is a fairly close parallel to Pluto in Gemini, and here we have one indication of the ferocious, ruthless and highly primitive aspects of the dictator's mind.

The conjunction of Neptune and Pluto in Gemini in the 8th is not conducive to real mental strength, but too much stress must not be laid upon a feature such as this, since it must have been common to many thousands of maps of this period.

Probably the key to the mental states lies with Moon conjunction Jupiter in the 3rd in Capricorn which gave a mind at one and the same time limited (by the uncongenial Saturnian sign) and expansive in the direction of material ambitions. Saturn, the dispositor, is in the 10th, and the Moon rules the 9th, the house of ideals.

That Hitler was, in some respects, a very gifted man mentally seems to be attested by several, at least, of his generals, and it may be affirmed that, had this Moon-Jupiter conjunction fallen, let us say, in Libra or Aquarius, and had the times been more propitious, he might have been a harmless, or even an admirable, idealist, in a true sense.

But Saturn controls this map, for not only does it dispose of two important bodies, but it squares Venus, which disposes of three more, and Mars, which disposes of yet another.

One may truly say that the native, in this case, hated the planet that held him in its grip. Hence his intense dislike of his father, of the Jews, of the Russians—all ruled by Saturn. Hence, too, below a superficial self-control, a terrible resentment of control (again, Saturn) which threw him into paroxysms of anger and hysterical weeping when his "unconscious" gained the upper hand.

Saturn rules the 4th and Hitler's early environment was very hostile to a normal development of character. The map is terribly limited, but there is in it the tremendous expansive force of the Moon with Jupiter and the catastrophic squares of Saturn to Mars and Venus, brooking no restriction. Mercury is opposed to Uranus, though somewhat weakly, and, as we have said, the mundane emplacement of Uranus tends to the neurotic.

The last degrees of Libra are, perhaps, not fortunate on the ascendant, for this brings into the 1st house a powerful Scorpio element (all the more so, as the two rulers are conjoined) and no two signs could be less congenial than Libra and Scorpio.

What charm and gentleness Hitler manifested can only be ascribed to the Venus degrees upon the radical Ascendant but by progression during most of his life Scorpio was rising.

An important point in this map is the position of the conjunction of Mars and Venus almost precisely between the Sun and Neptune. These last two are in semi-sextile, normally a weak contact. But the positions of Mars and Venus form with it a construct of considerable importance.[1]

Hitler's extreme ability as a liar, and not merely this, but his power of getting people to place faith in his lies—in a word, his plausibility—is perhaps best seen in the Libra-Capricorn combination, which is excellent for diplomatic work, though of course by no means necessarily dishonest. But in this horoscope Saturn and Neptune are in parallel, and there is a biquintile of Moon-Jupiter to Neptune, for what this may be worth. It may perhaps be admitted that the absence of a clear and strong Neptune affliction in this map is somewhat surprising.

Destiny.—This, to some extent, has been already touched upon, for one cannot mention character without referring to early surroundings.

That Hitler's career would lead to violence and conditions of stress and strain and bloodshed seems obvious enough. That he would end catastrophically is also plain for all to see, for Saturn in the 10th traditionally raises up and brings down again, unless very well placed—and here it is far from that. Why he should have ever risen so high is not quite so clear, if we take this geniture—as we are perforce now doing—in isolation, that is to say without referring to such things as the horoscope

---

[1] Formations such as this, when several bodies are spread out at equal intervals, have been called by the author "fans". One of the commonest arises when bodies are in trine and another body being exactly between them, is in sextile to both.

of Imperial Germany and the various mundane maps which have bearing upon the unfoldment of 20th-century history in Europe. For eminent men do not always show unmistakable signs of eminence in their horoscopes, since 'no man liveth unto himself alone', and it is the relation between the individual figure and those that have a collective effect that frequently yields the unmistakable indication.[1]

The death is well shown by the planets in the 8th, of which one is the strange Neptune which throws mystery around whatever it touches. In any case, the lords of the 4th and the 8th are violently afflicted, so that, given the times in which the native lived, an end amid blood and ruin was by no means unlikely.

Of his sexual life little is known with certainty, but the heavy afflictions to Venus indicate that this must have been far from fortunate. Venus with Mars, so near cusp 8, is not a bad indication of marriage almost in the moment of death.

As for his childlessness, this follows logically enough from the Saturnian dominance. Also, it is noteworthy that no body is placed in water, the fruitful element according to tradition.

In Hitler's case the outward life corresponded well enough to the inner.

As a second example, contrasting with the first, we give the nativity of the Florentine reformer, Savonarola, the authenticity of which ther is no reason to doubt. On the contrary, it i a very clear index to the life and chatacter of the native. The positions are given to the nearest degree only.

Here we find the Venus element very strong, through the sign of Libra, but the external nature, shown by the asc., is Martian, so that we get a rough exterior, but much idealism behind it.

---

[1] Of course other people must have been born with maps very like Hitler's, though not necessarily anyone with an *identical* geniture. The comparison of these cases of "astrological twins", when accurate cases are available, is of the greatest value as a means of investigating to what extent the "whole man" appears in the horoscope.

Five bodies are in air, two in earth, and two in water, while the asc. is in fire. One would not expect to find fire the weakest element of the four, but its importance is greatly stressed by the conjuction of Mars with the Moon. It is the horoscope of one who is a dreamer, but who will also come to the front and try to externalize his visions, for Mars always tries to bring things down to the concrete. Moreover, in this horoscope all the bodies except Jupiter are cardinal and most of them angular.

The Moon, conjoined to Mars and square Saturn, must have made the nature austere, fanatical, and turbulent, despite the strong Venus element and the profound sympathies shown by Jupiter in Pisces in the 12th trine Uranus in Cancer.

The position of the Moon also fully accounts for the reformer's desperate struggles with those in authority, shown by Saturn, lord of the 10th. The ruler exalted in the 10th raised him up and enabled him to maintain his position for a time, but Saturn in the 7th (open enemies) and ruling the 11th and 12th (friends and secret enemies) threw him down. It is likely that his friends betrayed him, and it cannot be questioned that he must have resorted too readily to extremes of language, if not of action.

The numerous planets in Libra in the 7th seem to show that the life was largely in the hands of others, despite the vigorous Martian personality. Both Venus and Jupiter are in their own signs, and the nature must have contained much that was sweet and gentle beneath a rough and perhaps uncouth exterior. But the monk was ill-advised, speaking from a wordly point of view, to leave a life of seclusion, for the fiery planets, which have so much to do with all that is public and manifest, are not strong. The Sun is in its fall and conjuction Neptune, without good aspects; Mars is prominent, but square Saturn; and Jupiter is cadent and in watery sign.

The terrible end of the reformer is clearly shown by the afflictions to the Moon.

CHAPTER NINE

PERSONAL APPEARANCE

THE influence of the horoscope upon the physical appearance of the native is one of the most interesting branches of Astrology.

The principal factor in the determination of this matter is the ascending degree, together with all planets in close aspect with it, and the signs containing them.

A planet on the M.C. will also affect the appearance, especially if in aspect with the asc.; and any satellitium, or group of planets conjoined in one sign, will leave a mark.

The influence of the luminaries may often be traced, and is sometimes powerfully marked, especially if one is on an angle.

A setting planet is important, as being in aspect with the asc., and it occasionally happens that the native's appearance is better described in terms of a setting planet and its sign than by the asc. itself.

Cardinal Signs tend to produce a rather tall, straight, moderately thin body, Aries being often scraggy, Cancer medium, Libra plump, and Capricorn lank.

The head is generally round in Aries and Libra, somewhat longer in Capricorn, but with marked cheek-bones, and rather broad, with a pointed chin, in Cancer.

Fixed Signs produce a heavy, solid build, broad shoulders, and an upright carriage.

The head is usually square, with a strong jaw and chin.

Mutables are inclined to be round-shouldered, often have loose lips and half-open mouths, and, except Pisces, are seldom fleshy.

They have the oval type of face, and usually small chins, but good foreheads.

The typical appearance of the signs may be briefly outlined:

Aries.—A quick, sharp, wide-awake appearance; there are two distinct types, one with a rather Red Indian physiognomy, the other with a round head, short snubbed nose, and aggressive chin. This type is usually short-sighted and pushes its head forward, often wearing pince-nez. The hair is usually reddish, sometimes dark; the body spare and wiry; the eyes grey or hazel. The demeanour is energetic.

Taurus.—A slow, deliberate, ponderous manner and a heavy, solid build, inclining to stoutness. The features are good, often there is much beauty of what is called the Irish type. Blue eyes, soft brown hair, red cheeks, and even teeth. The walk is measured, and the whole demeanour of the slow and sure kind.

Gemini.—Generally a light build, with quick, restless eyes, usually brown or hazel. The appearance is often dapper, and indicates intellectuality and mental acquisitiveness.

The demeanour is mobile, discursive, and discontinuative; quick notice is taken, and then the attention darts to something else.

Cancer.—Often a rather anxious expression, a kindly and sympathetic smile; the physical appearance is seldom robust or vigorous, and often the timidity and sensitiveness of the sign is very visible in the appearance, which is rarely "distinguished". At the same time it varies much with the Moon-position. The eyes are generally light in colour, the complexion and hair pale, the chin pointed, and the nose tilted and also pointed. The eyes are commonly small and deep.

Leo.—This also varies greatly with the solar position. Sun rising in Leo gives a fine, strong, robust man or woman, very broad, large open face and large, rather staring eyes. The complexion is florid and at times apt to be streaked. The hair, as in all fiery signs, inclines to thinness and a light colour.

Other types of Leo are often quite slim and active, and are recognizable chiefly by a long, rather pendulous nose.

Leo has a noticeable liking for dressing in furs, and altogether spends a good deal on dress and appearances.

The demeanour is friendly and jovial, at times self-important.

Virgo.—A neat, precise, scholarly, or clerkly appearance, well formed, and often well set up. The tendency to stoop is less than in the other mutables. The complexion is sallow and often muddy; the hair and eyes are brown. The demeanour usually impresses one as careful, matter-of-fact, and modestly competent, but the sign sometimes produces a good deal of conceit.

Libra.—Blue eyes, fair hair, and a fair, often pale complexion. The build is moderate in height, slight in youth, and putting on flesh in later life, when there is a marked tendency to develop a blotchy complexion. Sometimes the hair is golden; at other times it is light brown.

The demeanour is sociable, friendly, and happy.

Scorpio.—A thick-set, strong frame; sallow, olive, or dark red complexion, and hair often black and curly. The nose is prominent and aquiline, and usually thick in the nostrils. Often very muscular. The eyes are dark brown, and often possess a reddish glint. The chin is small but strong, and the face gaunt.

Red- or sandy-haired types, with steel-blue eyes, are sometimes seen.

The demeanour is either reserved and dignified, or, in low types, surly and rough.

Sagittarius.—Inclined to tallness, athletic, and vigorous, but sometimes stoop. A well-cut, high-bridged nose, fresh complexion, and thin light hair. The face is oval. Eyes grey or blue.

The demeanour is frank, friendly, fidgety, and restless, often with much loquacity.

Capricorn.—Usually tall and loose-jointed. Dark hair, lantern-jawed, long straight nose, white complexion and dark eyes. The beard is always sparse. The skin tends to crease and form folds. At times a peculiar sidelong glance.[1]

The demeanour is either solemn and rather formal, and stilted towards inferiors, or else pushful and anxious to be taken notice of.

Aquarius.—A well-formed, upright build, and handsome open expression; often good-looking, but tends to pallor. The cheeks are commonly pinched. Hair light brown, and the eyes either brown or greenish-brown. The head is usually large and square. The demeanour is sociable, unassuming, and quiet.

Pisces.—Often rather heavily and clumsily built, with bright complexion, brown eyes and hair. The features are inclined to be loose and fleshy; the nose is aquiline, but less finely cut than that of Sagittarius. The eyes are large and protrusive, often bagged. Shoulders are round and the gait rather rolling. Some types are extremely beautiful, and possess much spirituality and a far-off expression; in lower forms this is represented by a look of anxiety or perplexity.

The demeanour is very subject to moods—alternately full of fun, and then relapsing into depression and worry.

It will be perceived from the above descriptions that the question of personal appearance is a difficult though fascinating one. It is not uncommon to meet fairly typical examples of a sign, but more often a person presents an almost unrecognizable blend from which it is not easy to pick out even one prominent planetary influence. Again, it must be borne in mind that racial heredity necessarily enters largely into the question: a Mongolian is always a Mongolian under whatever configuration he may be born, and in England, where there is a

---

[1] The text-books usually paint an unprepossessing portrait of ♑, yet handsome examples are by no means unknown!

great diversity of racial characteristics, judgment becomes extremely complicated. To get an absolutely pure type it would be necessary to find a person born in a town and country ruled by his own ascending sign, whilst his own nativity should have the ruler rising in its own sign without powerful aspects either to itself or to the asc. degree, and no other sign or planet should occupy a prominent part of the map.

Some students lay great stress on decanate influence.

We have also seen that there are often distinct subtypes of signs, which do not seem to depend either on decanate or the position of the ruler, so that it is easy to produce two Leos, for example, that hardly have a visible feature in common, and yet would be instantly identified by an experienced student.

The end of the sign on the ascendant often produces a fairly true type if the following sign is not tenanted, but when the first one or two degrees of a sign are rising, the preceding sign, which has just left the asc., is of importance as regards both appearance and character.

PROGNOSTICATION

§ 1

PROGNOSTICATION involves three classes of planetary positions:

1. *Current* or those for the actual time in question.
2. *Radical*, or those of the nativity.
3. *Progressed*, or the actual positions of the planets for some time subsequent to birth which are found to operate, according to certain time-measures, at a later time in life.

These can obviously be combined in several ways. If we denote them by the letters C, R, and P we can get:

1. C + C. These are the different positions taken up by the planets from day to day without reference to any individual horoscope. They do not as a rule greatly affect the individual, but operate through races and masses of people. However, the movements of one's current ruling planet through signs and its passing from stationary to retrograde may produce noticeable effects of a minor character.
2. C + P, and C + R. The passage of any current body over a sensitive point in the progressed or radical horoscope is called a *Transit*. These are of considerable importance.
3. P + R, and P + P. It is by means of these that most prognostication is accomplished. There are two main systems of progression, called Primary and Secondary.

4. R + R represent, of course, the ordinary radical aspects. These may at first sight appear to have no connection with prognostication, but in point of fact no opinion could be more mistaken. *It is a cardinal rule that no direction can bring to pass what is not shown in the nativity.* Exceptions to this are virtually non-existent. The radical horoscope limits the operation of directions inexorably, and the latter only bring to manifestation what is already promised by the former. Hence a real understanding of the radix is a necessary forerunner of all successful attempts to look into the future. The radix shows what will happen; the directions, when.

§ 2. Transits, Lunations, Revolutions, and the Diurnal Horoscope

The importance of transits varies according to the radical strength of the planets or points involved and the speed of the transiting planet. A slow-moving planet is far more potent than a quick one, such as Mercury or Venus. These latter may, indeed, be as a general rule almost disregarded, but the transits of ♄, ♅, ♆ and Pluto are often very significant of events.

The effect of transits is most noticeable when they act as stimuli to a coincident direction.[1] This Law of Excitation, which is one of the most useful and exact in Astrology, may be thus stated:

"If at the time that a progressed body is in aspect to another by direction, either of these bodies forms an aspect by transit with either of the two directional bodies, then this transit will excite the direction into immediate operation."

---

[1] Direction is the name applied to the P to P or P to R aspects. Transits are not directions. To "direct" a planet it so move it, according to one of the systems of progression to be explained later, to form an aspect with another.

Thus, if the progressed Sun in 0° Cancer is trine Jupiter in 0° Scorpio, then any transit of the Sun or Jupiter over any point in aspect with 0° Cancer or 0° Scorpio will cause the direction to act.

It will be seen that, according to this statement of the law, the exciting body must be one of the two directional bodies. In our example, a transit of any other body except the Sun or Jupiter would not act as an excitant. This is in accordance with the writer's experience; excitation by planets other than those in direction is far less certain and powerful.

It will be seen that this law enables the student to determine, often within a day, when a direction will operate. At the same time it explains the frequent concern of beginners in Astrology who find one transit acting with great power and another with very little. The reason is that in one case the transit is a spark that ignites a direction; in the other it is a spark only.

Transits to R positions are usually regarded as more important than those to P places, but transits to the P positions of the heavy planets are often strong and perhaps this is particularly the case in later life, when the R positions may tend to "fade out" in favour of the P positions.

Special attention should be paid to the *stationary positions* of the planets, as, when these fall exactly on a sensitive place in the nativity, important characteristic results will follow.

Attention should also be paid to *simultaneous transits to the same point*, as when two bodies, in conjunction, are on a radical sensitive point, or two bodies are in some other aspect to a radical point. Such configurations vary in importance in accordance with the rules outlined above, but, if very close to the radical place, they deserve attention.

Important results may also follow two or more distinct transits occurring at the same time and being of more or less similar natures.

A special class of transits comprises *the passage of planets through houses.*[1] These may occupy considerable time, from an average of two and half days in the case of ☽ to an average of fourteen years in the case of ♆. They are often highly significant of the main trend of affairs during the period, so far as the house in question is concerned. If a powerful direction coincides in time and nature, the result will be very marked.

In judging the effect of these transits, much regard must be paid to the radical relationship between planet and house. If, for example, the former were in good aspect with the ruler or occupant of the house in the nativity, transit through the house would be the more powerful and benefic. If there were no connection at all, it would be far less noticeable.

Mars causes the matters of the house to be active; the native's attention is drawn to them and his energies directed to that department of his life. Disputes may arise, but progress is also very possible.

Jupiter causes progress, growth, prosperity, and pleasure by its passage through a house, but if badly afflicted at birth there may be loss through overhopefulness, recklessness, waste, and ostentation, or through the matters ruled by the houses over which the planet is lord.

Saturn causes increase of responsibility, even if strong, and brings about consolidation, a settling-down of conditions, or the establishment of affairs on a permanent basis. It may also show hardship, loss, bereavement, and opposition.

Uranus brings unexpected changes, sometimes leading to new conditions of great value, sometimes to loss of time and energy in pursuing false trails, and sometimes to disruptions. In mental houses it widens the mind and opens it to new influences and points of view.

Neptune causes chaos, worry, illness, and sometimes treachery, delusive conditions, or moral breakdown. If very strong it

[1] Often called ingresses. Domal transits seems a better term.

may cause gain, something after the manner of Jupiter, and, in watery houses, occult experiences.

The quicker planets do not stay long enough in a house to permit of their effects being very strongly felt. On the other hand, Uranus, Neptune and Pluto move so slowly that their effects are also not always noticeable, except in long perspective.

Eclipses and Lunations.—These are astronomically the same, except that in the case of an eclipse the Moon has little or no latitude, and so, at the time of ☌ or ☍, it is in a straight line with the Earth and Sun. Thus, by intervening between us and the Sun, it obscures the latter and occasions a solar eclipse, total or partial as the case may be. Or, by passing exactly behind the Earth, it is immersed in our shadow, and so suffers total or partial eclipse itself.

An annular eclipse of the Sun is similar to a total eclipse, except that, owing to the Moon's being unusually far from us at the time of obscuration, it is too small to cover the Sun's disc exactly and a ring of light is seen round the lunar orb.

An ordinary Lunation is a new or full Moon, and occurs when the Moon has too much latitude, north or south, to be in a direct line between ourselves and the Sun, and so cause an eclipse.

New Moons are important if they fall on sensitive parts of the nativity or progressed horoscope. Their effects generally appear about four days before the actual day of new moon.

Full Moons are less important, but if they fall on a sensitive place their effects will be noticeable.

Eclipses act similarly, but more powerfully, and, under excitation by a transit, their action may be observed months after their occurrence. Falling on benefics they act well, on malefics ill, and on the Lights, Mercury, or the angles, according to their strength in the radical. It must be borne in mind that an eclipse or lunation is really a simultaneous transit of the lights, and the effects must be judged with due regard to the radical strength of the luminaries to one another and to the point or body which they are affecting in the horoscope. If the Sun and Moon are both in affliction with the radical Jupiter, for example, their conjunction on that body by lunation or eclipse will effect little good. It would in fact bring into action whatever trouble the radical afflictions betokened by sign and house.

Eclipses, if falling on a radical or progressed planet, are thought by some to exert great power and rank equally with almost any direction.

On the other hand, neither lunation nor eclipse will produce much effect if more than 2° from a sensitive point.

They both act as very powerful stimuli under the Law of Excitation. There can, indeed, be no more potent stimulus of a solar or lunar direction than an eclipse falling on either of the directional bodies.

Eclipses that fall near the North Node (Caput) are said to be favourable and those that fall near the South Node (Cauda) to have the contrary propensity.

It must be noted that what are called eclipses in the almanac may be invisible in England. Indeed, a total solar eclipse is a rare event with us. In all cases the greater the degree of obscuration the more powerful the effect.

The Winter Ingress

The map for each winter ingress, year by year, is of great value as a general indication, so far as a single map can be such, of the events of the ensuing twelve months, regard being had to the transits shown in the map to the geniture in question.

Thus, Mars in the winter ingress on the Sun in Sagittarius in the natus might denote the possibility of a fractured femur, and so forth.

In the same way the entry of the Sun into the other signs (especially the three other cardinals) may yield interesting results.

The Capricorn ingress, however, is of paramount significance.

Solar and Lunar Revolutions

A figure cast for the time when the Sun by transit returns to its exact[1] radical place is considered in relation to itself and to the radix, and is deemed significant for the ensuing year.

A similar lunar revolution can be calculated for each month.

Another method is based on the return of the Moon, each month after birth to the same distance, or *elongation*, from the Sun, progressing each body. Each of these months is said to equal a year of life. These figures are called Synodical Returns.

In order to calculate exactly when the Sun will reach its radical place it is necessary to multiply 1440 (the number of minutes in a day) by the distance between its position at noon and the radical position, reduced to seconds of arc, and to divide the product by the distance travelled by the Sun on the day in question, also reduced to seconds of arc. The answer will be in minutes of time.

Or, using Chambers's Mathematical Tables, the operation can be done by ternary proportional logarithms. In this case the first term is the arithmetical complement of the distance travelled in the day, the second is the constant log. of 24 hrs., i.e., 87506. The answer will be in hours and minutes.

The same method is equally applicable to the calculation of ingresses or any problem involving the time taken for a moving body to reach a given point, its motion in 24 hrs. being known and also the distance to be traversed.

The Diurnal Horoscope

This is a modern introduction. A figure is erected for the day under consideration, using the sidereal time of that day and the same time of birth as for the nativity. That is to say, it is erected as if the native were re-born every day at the same hour a.m. or p.m. as was actually the case.

Such a figure, cast for any birthday, will, of course, nearly resemble the radical map so far as the houses are concerned. Then, with each additional day after the birthday, the angles will progress according to the increment in the sidereal time at noon on each successive day.

Such figures are said to be of use in determining the day

---

[1] i.e. to the nearest second of arc. Calculation to the nearest minute is insufficient.

when a direction will operate, and it is supposed that the coming of a planet on to an angle in the diurnal map will produce marked results.

§ 3. SECONDARY DIRECTIONS

It will be convenient to treat these before Primaries on account of their greater simplicity and the fact that they are in much commoner use.

They are based on the rule that *the planetary configurations subsequent to birth produce results in the life according to a time measure of one day equals one year*. That is to say, each day after birth represents a year of the life. Consequently, each hour equals about a fortnight.

It will thus be seen that a slight uncertainty as to the time of birth does not materially affect this system.

The study of secondaries presents little difficulty. The method is to erect a map for each day after birth, using the new sidereal time for that day and the same time, a.m. or p.m. as the case may be, as was used in erecting the nativity itself. Of course the progression is continuous, and no map will represent exactly more than the moment to which it corresponds in accordance with the time measure, but by erecting a map for each day (= year) it is easy to see what the intermediate positions will be.

Each successive map will show a progression of the Sun, Moon, and planets, and also the M.C. will advance about one degree, whilst the other houses will also advance, as shown in the table of houses for the place in question.

The progressed bodies will all form directions, from time to time, to other progressed bodies (since they all move at different rates) and to the various radical positions. Thus we have P to P and P to R directions, of which the latter are usually the more marked in action.

It may be observed that some writers on Secondaries (or, as they are sometimes called, Arabian directions) do not move the houses at all from their radical positions, arguing that such movement, being due to the axial rotation of the earth, is in reality primary. The system taught here is properly known as *The Progressed Horoscope*, and is a popular and convenient method which unites the whole of the Secondary System with important elements (i.e., the progression of the cusps) from the Primary.

Let us now consider, as an example, a person born in London at 6 p.m., January 1, 1924.

We erect the nativity. The S.T. at noon on day of birth = 18 hrs. 39 m. 30 s., to which add 6 hrs. 1 min., which gives a radical M.C. of 11° 0′ Aries.

Now, from the moment of birth, the planets and houses, move. If we want to see how they stand after one day, i.e. one year of life, we erect a map for 6 p.m. on 2nd January. The S.T. is now 0 hr. 44 m. 26 s., or a progression of 3 m. 56 s., which gives an M.C. of 12° 5′ Aries, while the planetary positions must all be recalculated, and, except Neptune, who is retrograde, have all moved forward.

We continue erecting similar maps for each day after birth.

The tabulation of directions must now be considered. These may be classified as follows:

a. Aspects formed by the Sun p. to all bodies p. and r. and asc. r. and M.C. r.

b. Aspects formed by the asc. p. and M.C. p. to all radical bodies.

c. Aspects formed by all p. bodies except the Lights and Angles to the radical Lights and Angles.

d. Interplanetary aspects p. to r. and p. to p.

e. Aspects by the Moon p. to all bodies p. and r.

f. Planets becoming stationary in the progressed (or regressed) horoscopes.

g. Lunations in the progressed or regressed map.

Of these *a* and *b* are most important and cover the chief events and stages of life. Owing to their comparatively slow motion they are not numerous, and can be soon tabulated.

c. These are usually less important, especially directions to radical angles. However the progression of a *slow-moving* planet to the exact aspect, especially the conjunction or opposition, of a radical angle or to the radical Sun or Moon, is an immensely powerful direction, all the more so because in such cases the bodies will probably have been in aspect at birth.

d. These are omitted by some writers, but this attitude is not recommended. At the same time mutual or interplanetary directions, as they are called, often effect little unless an appropriate lunar direction concurs.

e. These are valuable because, although they do not often indicate important events of themselves, yet if they coincide in nature with more powerful indications operative at about the same time, they act as "minute hands" to the horoscopic watch and often point to the exact day of incidence. When they are not backed by other and stronger progressions, their effects are weak and transient, often lasting but a few days.

f. and *g.* These are very important, especially if they form close aspects with radical or progressed or regressed bodies.

Progressed lunations, in such cases, extend their general influence until the next lunation is formed.

Note that the influence of such regressed lunations extend *up to the time they are formed*, after which the next lunation takes over.

Aspects formed by the progressed Sun or angles are often significant of lasting epochs in the life and may extend their influence over two or three years, coming into marked operation when excited by transits or secondary lunars. This is particularly true when progresion is made to the r. and p. positions of a slow-moving planet, at an interval of perhaps two or three or several years.

Directions to progressed positions are sometimes said to be less powerful than those to radical, but this may well vary with the individual, and the student should form his own opinion.

A particularly powerful class of direction arises when two bodies that are in contact in the natal chart complete that contact a considerable time later. In certain conditions this may measure to a period quite late in life. For example, the author (born 31st January, 1887) had Neptune in square to Venus, only about one degree apart. But Neptune was retrograde to stationary, after which it turned direct very slowly and did not complete the aspect for some 66 days (= years).

The Calculation of Directions

In order to see during which month a direction becomes exact, it is only necessary to do a short sum.

1. If the direction is to a radical position, find how far the moving body has to go to make the aspect exact, using minutes. Multiply this by twelve and divide by its daily motion, also in minutes. The result gives the months after the birthday when the direction is exact. If, instead of twelve, you take 365 you get your answer in days.

Example.—In the case given on page 44, when will Sun ✶ Mars r. be exact? Mars r. = 18° 20′ ♏, so that ☉ must reach 18° 20′ ♑. On the 9th, at 6 p.m., it is at 18° 13′ ♑; therefore it has 7′ to go, and its daily motion is 61′.

Then 7 × 365 = 2,555, which divided by 61 gives about 42. It will, therefore, become exact about 42 days after the 8th birthday.

2. If the direction is to a progressed (i.e., moving) body, we must find out how much the directed body gains on the other in a day. Unless it does gain, it obviously cannot form the aspect at all. Then find out how much it is behind the complete aspect.

Then say: If it takes a day to gain so much, how long will it take to gain what it needs to complete the direction?

Example.—On January 23, 1924, at noon, the Sun is in 2° 13′ ♒ and ♂ in 2° 23′ ♐, and we see that at noon on the next day the Sun has passed the sextile. When was this ☉ ⚹ ♂ exact? Now the Sun's motion = 61′, and Mars' = 39′, i.e., the Sun gains 22′ in the day. And at noon it is 10′ from the exact aspect.

If it gains 22′ in the day (= dir. year) it will obviously gain 10′ in $\frac{10}{22}$ of that period.

We have selected a birth-time at noon for simplicity's sake, but that in no way affects the method.

After a little practice all times, except the Moon, can be detected to the nearest month by mere inspection of the ephemeris.

With the Moon it may be thought advisable to tabulate its monthly position by adding one-twelfth of its daily motion to its birthday position for each successive month. This enables aspects and the month of their being exact to be more readily detected.

It is often advisable to reckon lunar directions to the exact day by the foregoing method, using 365 instead of twelve, and so obtaining the answer in days.

Example.—On January 2, 1924, the Moon is conjunction Mars p.: when does this fall?

$$\text{Moon's motion} = 882'.$$
$$\text{Mars' motion} = 38'.$$

Therefore Moon's gain in day = 844′.

Moon is behind by 208′.

Then, if it gains 844′ in 265 days, in how many will it gain 208′?

$$\frac{365 \times 208}{844} = 90 \text{ days}$$

Lunar directions often produce their maximum results very punctually on, or just before, their exact date.

The student should adopt a methodical style in calculating directions, and should take them exhaustively planet by planet.

An excellent plan is to form, once for all, a table of your Places of Aspect. Go through the natus carefully, tabulating every point which is in any aspect with any planet. Then, when wishing to discover if any progressed body is near any aspect with the radix you need only glance at your table, and, provided it has been correctly drawn up, any oversight or omission is impossible. The initial labour is saved many times.

Progressed directions (p. to p.) are not shown in this way, but are given in modern ephemerides.

Parallels of declination are things apart, but can be worked out by the foregoing method, although perhaps they are best dealt with by means of a *graph*.

For this purpose procure squared paper and write in the degrees of declination, from 0° to 25°, on the left hand, with perhaps 2 lines between each, for thirds of a degree. Then let the vertical lines represent your birthdays for successive years. Again leave some lines between these for subdivisions of the year, according to the scale on which you wish to work.

Then, in red ink, rule across the sheet the radical declination of each body, marking beside each what it is. If two bodies have the same declination one line will serve for both. These lines will be exactly horizontal, since the radical declination remains unaltered.

Then, in pencil, plot the annual progressed declinations of each body. The Moon will form sharp curves, but the others will alter very little, and probably very regularly, so that you need hardly plot them for each year. Uranus and Neptune will deviate very little from their radical line.

Wherever two lines intersect, a progressed par. dec. aspect is shown, and the vertical line will indicate the time of operation, more or less exactly according to the scale of the graph.

By these means the par. dec. aspects of a lifetime can be tabulated in an hour or so.

Those who are fond of such methods can extend them to other branches of Directional Astrology.

The Adjusted Calculation Date

This is a labour-saving device well worth mastering.

Refer to the example on page 165.

Since birth was six hours (= a quarter of a day) *after* noon, noon itself must correspond to a quarter of the year, or three months, *before* birth. It will, therefore, be perfectly legitimate to work always with the *noon positions*, copied straight out of the ephemeris without any calculations, at the same time dating everything not from the birthday, but from an Adjusted Calculation Date, which is to the birthday as noon is to the time of birth.

Thus if a person were born at noon his birthday and A.C.D. would coincide; if he were born two hours before noon, noon would equal one month after the birthday, and so on throughout the twenty-four hours.

This, of course, applies to the Sun, Moon, and planets, but not to the houses, which (unless adjusted) will continue to refer to the birthday.

Pre-Natal Secondary Directions or Regressions

These are calculated in exactly the same manner as ordinary post-natal secondaries, but are reckoned backwards instead of forwards, so that the twenty-four hours immediately *before* birth correspond to the first year of life, and so on.

On the whole they appear to be less reliable and less important than post-natal directions. No certain conclusions have been arrived at as to whether the events that accompany them differ in kind from those indicated by other classes of direction and, if so, in what respect.

Planetary Periods

At this point it is appropriate to mention the fact that each planetary influence tends to be active at a certain period in human life rather than at others. This scarcely belongs to the study of directions properly so-called, and yet it often explains the sweeping changes that sometimes come over a person's fortunes, and, to some extent, the disposition as well.

The Moon rules infancy. As the child learns to run and talk he comes under Mercury, and this persists till puberty or later, gradually giving way to a greater or less extent to Venus. This is followed about the age of 25 by the period of the Sun, when the native takes his place in public life and begins to make his mark in life, if at all. Then comes the Mars period, from 41 to about 56. Then that of Jupiter, when the purely physical activities of the Sun and Mars begin to wane, and the mind and emotions are broadened, whilst the life settles down to comfort if the earlier activities have been successful. Lastly, Saturn rules from about 68 onward into old age.

Uranus is thought by many to rule extreme longevity. Neptune perhaps rules senility.

These periods vary greatly according to the nativity. A very Saturnian person will be dominated by that planet all his life, for good or ill as the case may be. But its clearest manifestation will be during the Saturnian period, and so with the others.

§ 4. PRIMARY DIRECTIONS

These are based on the *apparent* motion of the heavenly bodies immediately after birth, no account being usually taken of their proper motion.

The time-measure is the passage of one degree of *right ascension*[1] over the mid-heaven of the horoscope, which is taken

---

[1] This is the "classic" method, but the author finds that the addition of one degree of longitude is not only much simpler, but at least as accurate Others may prefer the "radix measure" increment (see below) of 59′ 8″ a year.

to equal one year of the life. As one degree passes over the M.C. in about every four minutes of time, it will be seen that this measure is very rapid, and a slight error in time will throw many of the directions out by many months. For example, twenty seconds equal a month. The rapidity of the measure also explains why no notice is generally taken of the *proper* motions of the planets: ninety years of life only equal six hours of time, and in this period most of the planets move very little. Nevertheless it seems that account may be taken of the proper motion of the Moon, and even of the Sun, Mercury, Venus, and Mars, and direction may be made logically and successfully both to their radical and progressed positions.

Primaries are considered to denote above all matters of fate or destiny, while having small influence on the development of thought and character. They are therefore of great importance in judging accidents and other matters over which the native has little or no control.

Their calculation involves time and care, and more than the average aptitude for mathematics, and their consideration is usually included only in specialized textbooks. Yet their importance forbids their entire omission.

It is usual to calculate only those primaries that involve what are called the Significators, i.e., Sun, Moon, M.C., and Asc. These are directed, or moved, to the places of other bodies or to the significator itself. Thus, we have always a *preceding* body or place of aspect, which is considered as remaining stationary in its radical place in the heavens, and we have a *succeeding* body or place of aspect which is brought to it.

All ordinary primaries are really converse, because they are formed by apparent motion, which is always converse to the zodiac.

Interplanetary primaries are effective, but are not always used.

The coming of bodies or places of aspect on to the angles gives us directions to these points, and these are easily calculated.

In order to reckon primary directions to the M.C. it is necessary to get a table showing the R.A. corresponding to the zodiacal degrees, with latitude, and then to convert into R.A. the radical M.C. and the degree of the place of aspect. The difference will give the arc of direction, which turn into time at the rate of one year for each degree and one month for each five minutes.

To calculate the asc. is harder, but this may be correctly done by finding the R.A. of the M.C. when the place of aspect rises, and then directing the radical M.C. to this second M.C. as if it were an M.C. direction. Needless to say, for these directions positions must be taken to the minute.

Solar primaries seldom differ much in point of time from the corresponding secondaries, but lunar primaries are a class by themselves. Calculation of these two types of primaries, as well as of interplanetaries, is made by a proportional sum involving the semi-arcs and meridian distances of the two bodies and worked by logarithms.

The student is recommended to study primaries in such works as Zadkiel's *Grammar* (reprinted with Lilly's *Introduction*), but unfortunately many differences of opinion exist as to theory and practice, and the whole subject is embarrassed by a very arbitrary terminology.

§ 5. "Symbolic or Fixed-Increment Directions

By this term are denoted all directions not based on any astronomical motion of the planets or houses.

Such directional methods have been in use since antiquity, and they have received renewed attention.

These measures have the advantage of extreme simplicity, and appear at least as satisfactory as the more difficult systems.

In all symbolic methods there is a fixed annual increment or progress, which is added to all factors, including the angles.

The principal measures are:

The *Radix Measure*, introduced by Dr. Gornold, which is the mean daily motion of the Sun (and is therefore not, in the fullest sense, symbolical). This motion is 59′ 8″ a year of direction, and tables are published to show the progress by this ratio in any given number of years and days.

Others prefer the *actual solar motion* at the rate of one day = one year, applying this to all bodies.

The present writer uses the radix increment which often dates very closely to time and tends to produce definite events. But he also employs a fixed increment of *one degree for every year* of life (the one degree or o-d measure), which seems more general in its effects than the radix, producing (usually at the time of exactitude and for some time afterwards) both events and conditions. In early life there is, of course, little difference between the dates of a given radix and o-d. but as time goes on this increases.

With these directions it seems that the actual time of precipitation is often indicated not so much by transits under the Law of Excitation as by current aspects between the bodies concerned. Thus for example, Mars square Mercury may be shown by an aspect in the heavens between these bodies.

A much slower measure often effective is $\frac{1}{4}°$ = one year. It seems to affect worldly status and prosperity and is often present at death.

W. Frankland has introduced the *Point of Life*, an imaginary point which starts in all maps at 0° Aries and progresses through the zodiac at the rate of one sign for every seven years, i.e., at $4\frac{2}{7}$th degrees a year, forming directions in doing so.

He has also suggested a measure of $\frac{4}{7}$ths of a degree = one year which Gornold declared should be $\frac{3}{5}$ths of a degree, the difference being slight. These are recommended for trial.

However, the student will realize that too lavish a use of these measures must result in chaos.

The ideal is "no event or condition without an appropriate direction and conversely no direction without an appropriate event or condition".

Unless at least an approximation to this is insisted upon, almost any system will seem to pass muster.

§ 6. RECTIFICATION

When the time of birth is not known, or is known only approximately, it is customary to endeavour to *rectify* the horoscope, or, in other words, to adjust it to a putative correct time.

If the hour is not known even approximately it may be possible to perform a rough rectification by considering the physical appearance, temperament, and fortunes of the native, a map for the day of birth being moved to and fro until it appears to conform to these data.

For example, if the native has undergone many unexpected financial losses Uranus may be moved into the 2nd, and a general examination will ensue as to how far this agrees in other respects with his life, as, for instance, does the condition of the 7th agree with his marriage experiences?

When a satisfactory preliminary adjustment has been made (or if the time has been approximately recorded) the determination of a more exact time of birth is comparatively simple.

This is usually done by the passage of planets over the angles by primary direction, as explained on pages 171–173. This method, however, is only possible in the case of adults.

We may see that our hypothetical map puts Jupiter in the 10th house, about 12° of R.A. from the M.C. We then ask: Did any event transpire about the age of 12 which would be in conformity with such a direction as M.C. ☌ ♃? If we find that it did not, but that such an event happened two years later, then we move the M.C. 2° back, and test again by some other direction. The more events we can use in this way, the better; and finally we strike an average from the several results we have obtained, so as to get the M.C. which gives the best mean result.

Further, the aspect of a planet to an angle by Secondary motion will often yield a good rectification.

The slower symbolical measures are useful for rectification, as also transits.

As time goes on a hypothetical time can be constantly tested, until it becomes practically certain.

§ 7. EFFECTS OF DIRECTIONS

It must always be borne in mind that the strength of directional contacts depends not so much on whether the particular aspect is a "strong" or a "weak" one as on the natal conditions affecting the bodies, expecially in their mutual relationship. For example, if two bodies are in conjunction at birth, the progressions even to a semi-sextile or quincunx may be important, and this seems particularly true of "symbolic" contacts.

Individuals differ greatly in what may be called their directional receptivity and in their response to special classes of directions. Some answer to almost every kind of transit and direction; others do so feebly and irregularly. A system which satisfies all does not seem to exist, or at least to have been discovered. Those who live a "full" life naturally respond more readily than those whose lives are governed by routine. Many strong close aspects in the radix point to ready responses, whereas weak horoscopes respond weakly.

Exact forecasts as to how a given direction will work out are scarcely possible, except perhaps when the reactions of the particular map in question are well understood as a result of long observation.

Horoscopes in which the mutable signs are prominent seem

in general more difficult subjects for prognostic work than others.

In accord with general principles, any direction, good or bad, tends to bring benefits or trouble through the things and people ruled by the bodies involved. Houses occupied and ruled (and here the radical, not the progressed, positions seem most marked) must be duly considered. But hardly any direction brings out *all* the possibilities that it contains, and it remains a difficult and intricate problem to decide which are likely to emerge most strongly. A knowledge of the actual circumstances that surround the subject is a great help.

Thus if a monarch be known to occupy a shaky throne, a direction such as Sun square Saturn might easily point to loss of royal authority; but if he ruled in stable conditions, then an increase in responsibilities and serious difficulties would probably be closer to the result, with personal problems of a Soli-Saturnian kind in terms of the houses ruled and occupied.

Often it happens that there is more than one indication of a like nature. Thus, in the case given above, it might be that the essential rulerships of the Sun and Saturn (houses 5, 10 and 11) might be reinforced by one of the two bodies occupying or ruling (accidentally) one of these houses and thus underlining its significance. The affairs of a house thus doubly stressed are by that much the more likely to figure conspicuously in the response.

The following general hints as to the effects of the planets in direction may be some guide:

The Sun

Affects the broad unfoldment of the life on its active side, both exterior and intellectual. There is often an effect felt through the offspring. Physical vitality is augmented or the reverse as the case may be. May act through the father.

The Moon

Concerns everyday occurrences and general health. Domestic matters. May act through the mother.

Mercury

Covers relationships of all sorts, particularly those that depend upon writing and travel. One's correspondence. Examinations. Young people. Changes of thought and occupation. Mental stimulation, or, on the other hand, irritations and vexations. Often acts through relatives.

Venus

Relations with the other sex. Pleasure, holidays, enjoyment. Musical and artistic interests. Money-matters. Social life, and social adjustments.

Mars

Pain, or enhanced physical fitness and energy. Matters relating to death or the dead. Quarrels and accidents, acts of courage and daring.

Jupiter

New vistas and opportunities. Speculative thought; travel. Cheerfulness and good hopes, or, under affliction, temptations to take risks, gamble or waste money or energies. A progressive spirit, prudent or otherwise, as the case may be.

Saturn

A conservative spirit, retrenchment and consolidation of one's affairs and resources or, under affliction, disappointment and loss. Possiblity of diseases, especially such as are due to cold or want. Added responsibilities and burdens, often connected with the aged. A strong sense of duty and even a sense of inadequacy. Dealings with landed property.

Uranus

Unexpected developments, good or unfavourable as the nature of the contact and radical map may indicate. Dealing with officials and those in authority. A possibility of accidents, especially in relation to electrical devices. A propensity to act strangely and to be "unlike one's self". Romantic experiences.

Neptune

Nearly always, when the aspect is inharmonious, anxieties and worries, often over things that never happen. Experiences connected with gas, water, snow or ice, such as frozen pipes. Deceptive and tricky conditions. Drug-taking or alcoholic experiences, or contacts with people given to such things. Matters of art, music or drama, or persons related therewith, may enter the life. Sea-voyage or holidays by the sea, relations with hospitals, charities or prisons. Activity of the fantasy-forming propensity and day-dreaming.

Pluto

A resurrection of things past and half-forgotten. Death amongst one's connections. Probably an effect in terms of health and money. The opening and closing of "chapters" in the life. Feelings of solitude; isolation.

Duration of Directions

Secondary lunar directions are usually over and done with in a week or so of exactitude, conjunctions and oppositions lasting a little longer.

Interplanetary directions may be given a fortnight on each side of exactness but may be excited by lunars or transits somewhat sooner or later.

Fixed Increments appear seldom to act before exactness but may continue thereafter for two or three months.

Solar directions may last roughtly six months before and after exactitude.

Those directions (e.g., a retrograde Neptune coming by secondary motion to an aspect of a radical) which are very close over a long period do not actually appear to be in active operation in the life over a corresponding number of years.

All directions seem to act *after* rather than *before* their exact time of formation, but they are often close to that time.

When speaking of directions being in operation, it must be borne in mind that some directions produce lasting results, as for example marriage, the loss of a limb, and so forth. That does not mean, of course, that we can consider the direction which inaugurated this condition as being continuously in action.

Important developments are usually shown by a series of directions of like tendency and when this is the case it will not be easy to determine the principal time of precipitation.

CHAPTER ELEVEN

THEORETICAL CONSIDERATIONS

WE have now discussed the practical side of Natal Astrology in its entirety, and seen how the nativity is erected, progressed, and judged. The thoughtful reader will, however, find these studies not only interesting and useful in the highest degree in themselves, but also an extraordinary incentive to further and deeper investigation and thought.

It is not difficult to see that the phenomena of astrological science are different from those of physics, chemistry, and other branches of human knowledge which deal only with physical matter. It is true that many astrologers do seek to explain astrology in terms of physics. For example, the facts of wireless telegraphy are used as a basis for illustrating the nature of the influences which produce (as this school claims) the results known to astrology. But it seems clear that astrological facts are different from these. Sometimes we seem to encounter examples of direct effects, as for instance when a transit of Mars causes us to cut our finger, to lose our temper, or to act in some way on impulse. But how shall we explain, by any analogy drawn from physics, the equally indisputable fact that often a similar astrological indication results, not in our *doing* anything, but in our *becoming the objects* of the actions of others ? Thus, we may (to continue the above illustration) be cut by the careless act of another, be assailed by an individual who, through no behaviour of ours, has lost *his* temper, or suffer from the impulses of another. To take another case: it is held that Mars in close aspect to the ascending degree "causes" a propensity to red hair. But the fact that a child will have red hair is settled some time before birth and when, therefore, no ascendant exists. Again, there are the facts of directional and horary astrology, which, it is considered, point to something very different from the natural laws known to physical science. Another peculiarly interesting and radically important doctrine of astrology is the supreme significance of the *beginning of anything*, whether this law operates in respect of the nativity, of an inceptional figure, or in horary astrology.

Another school of astrologers attempts, to some extent, the explanation of astrological science by reference to the doctrines of occultism, though I am not aware that any efforts have been made from this quarter to give a comprehensive explanation of our problems.

This much must be universally conceded, that man, whether he is part of the Cosmos or is a distinct principle planted in it, as in a field for development, is certainly affected by it and in turn is able to act upon it. From the standpoint of his self-development it would obviously be without purpose to place man in the Cosmos unless this reciprocal action were possible.

But we do not call all the effects of the Cosmos that man encounters astrological; if he is soaked by the rain or drowned in the sea we do not call the action of rain or sea an astrological effect, but a purely physical one. Astrology, however, would give a sufficient reason why any individual, at any particular time, is brought into contact with the rain or with the sea, unless the results of such contacts were so trivial as to defy investigation.

Hence it seems that astrology is the science of certain subtle or occult relationships, which cannot be interpreted in terms of physical science, and cannot even be readily brought within the conception, fundamental in physics, of causation.

It is known, by the experiments of qualified scientific investigators, that there is a realm, call it what we will, in which phenomena take place that cannot be explained in terms of physical science—I refer to the phenomena usually called "psychic". I believe that the operations of the planets belong primarily, though not necessarily entirely, to that sphere, which is of a different order from the order of physics.

In this sense astrology may be justly called an occult or cryptic science.

When we turn, however, to the significance of the astrological factors, as distinct from the way in which they actually affect us, we reach a higher plane, and are dealing with Symbology. For the Sun, Moon, planets, signs, houses, and aspects unquestionably derive their meanings from cosmic principles, as I have endeavoured to explain elsewhere.[1]

With respect to the old question—Can a man rule his stars? Common sense would appear to indicate the reasonableness of taking ordinary care when directions are evil, and to make appropriate use of good influences. No one, unless incredulous as to the truth of astrology or wilfully careless, would choose to take a sea-voyage under an evil Neptunian direction; though it is fairly certain that such prudence would not entirely defeat the direction.

Besides taking such reasonable steps, various schools of thought have suggested means to nullify planetary influences. For example, talismans, amulets, and similar devices are used by many.

It is probable that courage and faith are more valuable than any such means, and that these, in fact, are valueless without such inner supports. The cultivation of such attitudes of mind stimulates the benefic action of Jupiter in our maps, and, if they do not remove tribulations, at least they help us to bear them.

Thus, though man cannot "rule his stars" in the sense of manipulating or twisting their effects to his own ends, he can

[1] *The Zodiac and the Soul*, published by the Theosophical Publishing House.

and should, lift himself above the sphere of their action by those methods which the great moralists of all time have inculcated. If the student places his true good in his intellect and reason he will not concern himself unduly over mundane success or failure, and he will try to lift others to the same elevation of thought. It is only the part of man that belongs to Nature which is susceptible of planetary effects but "there is a principle of the soul superior to all Nature, through which we are capable of surpassing the order and system of the world" (Iamblichus).

Man cannot, perhaps, 'conquer the stars' upon their own plane, but he is, by the intrinsic dignity of his being, superior to this plane; and he can at any time and at all times lift himself above its everchanging surface by the exercise of the spiritual faculties of his soul. This is the true "ruling of one's stars".

It is also the solution of the problem of fatalism so often raised in astrological discussion. For when man sees in all that happens to him or to others the irresistible tide of Providence, willing and accomplishing the highest good of all beings, he then consciously and gladly unites his will to the Divine Will: thus the seeming conflict between freedom and fate is finally resolved.

INDEX

187

SOME QUEST BOOK TITLES

AN ABRIDGEMENT OF THE SECRET DOCTRINE
by H. P. BLAVATSKY
edited by Elizabeth Preston and Christmas Humphreys

THE MEANING OF PERSONAL EXISTENCE
by ARTHUR W. OSBORN

THE MYSTERY OF HEALING
edited by Adelaide Gardner

REINCARNATION:
An East-West Anthology
by JOSEPH HEAD and S. L. CRANSTON

THE SCIENCE OF YOGA
by I. K. TAIMNI

SCIENTIFIC EVIDENCE OF THE
EXISTENCE OF THE SOUL
by BENITO F. REYES

THE TRANSFORMING MIND
by LAURENCE J. BENDIT and PHOEBE D. BENDIT

For a complete descriptive list of all Quest Books write to:

QUEST BOOKS
P.O. Box 270, Wheaton, Ill., 60187